Comhairle Contae
Átha Cliath Theas
South Dublin County Council

LIBRARY SERVICES ONLINE at www.southdublinlibraries.ie

Items should be returned on or before the last date below. Fines, as displayed in the Library, will be charged on overdue items. You may renew your items in person, online at www.southdublinlibraries, or by phone.

D0531410

Skymeadow

Notes from an English Gardener

CHARLIE HART

Constable • London

CONSTABLE

First published in Great Britain in 2018 by Constable
This paperback edition published in 2019

1 3 5 7 9 10 8 6 4 2

A CIP catalogue record for this book
is available from the British Library.

ISBN: 978-1-47212-876-8

Typeset in Sabon by Hewer Text UK Ltd, Edinburgh
Printed and bound in Great Britain by Clays Ltd, Elcograf S.p.A.

Papers used by Constable are from well-managed
forests and other responsible sources.

MIX
Paper from
responsible sources
FSC® C104740

Constable
An imprint of
Little, Brown Book Group
Carmelite House
50 Victoria Embankment
London EC4Y 0DZ

An Hachette UK Company
www.hachette.co.uk

www.littlebrown.co.uk

For Mummy & Daddy
and
Sybilla, of course

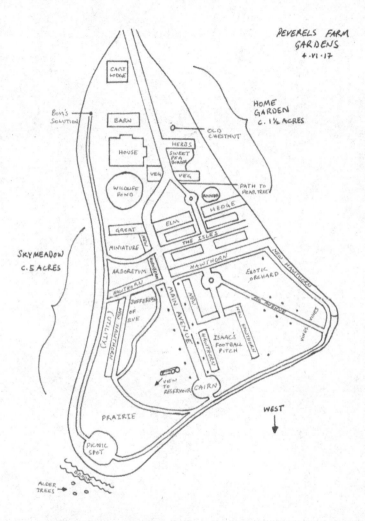

PEVERELS FARM
GARDENS
4·VI·17

HOME
GARDEN
C. 1½ ACRES

CART
LODGE

BIM'S
SOLUTION

BARN

OLD
CHESTNUT

HOUSE

HERBS

SWEET
PEA
BORDER

VEG   VEG

WILDLIFE
POND

PATH TO
PEAR TREE

HEDGE

ELM

GREAT

THE ISLES

MINIATURE

HAWTHORN

SKYMEADOW
C. 5 ACRES

ARBORETUM

HAWTHORN

NEW HAWTHORN

EXOTIC
ORCHARD

NEW HAWTHORN

SUFFERINGS
OF
EVE

MAIN AVENUE

NEW

NEW HAWTHORN

ZIG AVENUE

VINES VINES

(UTILITY)

NEW HAWTHORN

ISAAC'S
FOOTBALL
PITCH

NEW HAWTHORN

VIEW
TO
RESERVOIR

CAIRN

WEST

PRAIRIE

PICNIC
SPOT

ALDER
TREES →

Prelude

Here I have been slayed with wonder. Here I have been reminded of what it is to truly live, to stand on life, not grief or death. To reach inside a box of fear and find it empty. Here, a place whose essential character is cheeriness, a cheeriness so powerful it wells up and brims over and shares itself with the rest of the created order. Here I have built and here I have found myself in the building; here I have been able to join with Juliet and say,

> Nightly she sings on yon pomegranate-tree:
> Believe me, love, it was the nightingale.

Winter

A *first glimpse*

I am now three years and one herniated disc into creating the garden of our dreams but Sybilla and I remember our first visit to Peverels, arranged by the estate agent, as if it were yesterday. The moment we walked through the large oak door we had no qualms about the farmhouse – it is lovely. The ceilings aren't stratospheric in height and the walls could be a little thicker but it sits quietly and somehow lazily on the lip of a hill and its land runs from this lip down into the depths of the Peb Valley. But it wasn't the house that slayed us with wonder and sent me off to the mortgage broker; it was the seven acres of England that came with it.

From the first moment, we fell immediately into a sort of trance of admiration. Before turning off the engine, it was obvious that we had found a truly rural paradise unlike any other we had visited. The house sits in a garden, which itself sits in a vast sea of rolling East Anglian cornfields. There was (and is) no neighbour for half a mile or more, no view from the house that even partially made a concession to modernity.

We had been searching for an island without knowing it. Our lives had been steadily growing in noise, the noise of loss and grief, the noise of busyness, the noise that comes from the expectations of others; and for me the constant burr of not being able to feel through my work to the purpose that lay beneath it. On that first visit, the silence of the place struck us. Even in those first few hours we drank down the silence in great draughts. It was just what we needed.

I was grieving the death of my father and anxious about the impending death of my mother. In one corner of the garden I found two Scots pines that rushed towards the sky at a crazy tilt. They reminded me of my father. They reminded me of when he used to read me *Winnie-the-Pooh*. Piglet's innocent foolishness had been one of the first jokes we had truly shared together. As I stood in the garden I felt his pleasure.

We also knew that the only reason we might even have a chance to buy this Arcadia was because (unlike most English Arcadias) it didn't require the purchase of a mansion house along with it. And yet, as a place, it contained just enough of the two places in which we had ourselves grown up. Other than the areas immediately adjacent to the house the garden was a blank canvas. I knew immediately that I wanted to build a sumptuous large-scale garden. I started it that day in my mind as I drove back to London. I knew this was my chance. I knew in London I had only been playing at gardening. Still, large or small, our gardens, by merely being there each morning when we wake up, can somehow wrap themselves around us and help us face the tribulations of the outside world. Certainly ours have.

We left excited but anxious. I wondered whether I might not be replicating Piglet's innocent foolishness, but even if I was, there was already no turning back. Standing between us and any sort of reasonable conclusion to this instant love affair was the need to agree a price and extract a large mortgage from the bank, but I returned to London entirely determined to give everything I had to wrestling from the universe the only outcome that, to me at least, made any sense.

The garden

Even on our first visit to Peverels, it was plain that the garden had almost unlimited potential. Its range and scope would provide plenty of material, even for the most ambitious designer. The house is approached via a long, straight drive flanked on the left-hand side by hundred-foot poplar trees at intervals of twenty yards growing through a dense hedge of hawthorn, wild plum and hazel. The right-hand side delivers expansive views across the valley and down to a great reservoir. This side has no hedge but is planted with a mixed row of cherries, crab apples, Scandinavian maples and mountain ash; all unusual trees for an English approach. The drive itself is a thing of beauty and, as you turn into it, the trees on either side seem to touch above you, making an extended archway into another world; a living cloister, dense on one side, open on the other, and seemingly longer than any adjacent to a cathedral.

At the end of the drive you enter Peverels itself; here is the apex from which the sides of the plot gently open before tumbling happily down into the valley below. The boundaries are marked with thick hedges and mature trees of all types. Looking back at Peverels from the other side of the valley, you see a wooded triangular island on a hill with a white house somewhere among it. In high summer the trees provide a canopy of every type of green; from yellows and blues to acids and argents; all the greens that seem impossible to mix on a palette; all the greens you could ever want.

The space immediately adjacent to the house is itself a triangle sitting at the top of the larger triangle. It is comprehensively hedged and within it sits a cart lodge, a barn, an orchard, a pond and a garden – in short, all the paraphernalia necessary for when the house was an Elizabethan farmlette. This area I call the home garden and it is where the challenge of designing a garden within a triangle is most pronounced.

On that first visit, it was the area below the home garden that I eyed greedily. Below the great elm hedge was an expanse of almost virgin territory; the site for a new and audacious garden, one which would have avenues and rooms linked by clearly demarcated 'walks'. Here, there would be enclosed places for hiding juxtaposed against vistas that to me, at least, felt just as dramatic as the great Brownian ones. Just as dramatic despite the fact, perhaps because of the fact, that they were not contrived; they just were.

I could see, straight away, that as the plot stretched out down into the valley there could be a series of reveals, almost like terraces with the great elm hedge providing the first one. I noticed how well the roses grew, and one in particular, a huge Albertine on the northeast corner of the house. I knew already that roses loved Essex clay. So, by deduction, I knew that roses (and the whole rose family) would likely be the plant family that formed the core of any new garden we built. That was what I wanted because, of all the families of flora, Rosaceae contains the greatest number of plants that are of particular importance to me.

On that first visit, I had no clear idea about the detail of what I would build, but I knew the scope of my ambition and it was clear that if I managed to get close to making the sort of garden I dreamt of, it was going to take a lot of physical graft and, potentially, a lot of money.

Ground zero

It is not always easy to know the true genesis of something, but knowing where a thing starts often helps you to know the thing itself. This is self-evidently the case with words, but I think true also of people and their passions. Of course, this garden couldn't have happened if we hadn't moved out of London, it couldn't have happened if we hadn't moved here and it couldn't have happened without me. But none of these explain where the garden truly started; they just describe the effective causes. The garden really started three years before we moved, as I stood in a room in the West Suffolk Hospital, flanked by my two brothers as we witnessed our father take his leave for the final time.

He had been such an overarching and titanic figure in all of our lives. He was the sun around which we had all orbited. Not just us, but everyone in our household (which was large) and everyone on the farm, in fact most of the people in our lives generally, even our friends, even our detractors, even his detractors had somehow been caught by his gravity and were held in his orbit. If you had known our family at the time, you would know that my description is not all that hyperbolic.

My father had led a technicolour life. He was a sort of sun king. In fact, he slept in a giant bed with a crowned canopy within which sat a mirror with a vast gilded surround to look like the sun throwing out its light. He slept in a south-facing room with four double-height, giant windows that had the shutters thrown back, day or night, winter or summer. He had always been generous in the sense that anyone who happened to be in his orbit was permitted to bathe in his light. For all of us, the sun had taken its final pass.

Afterwards, I remember a feeling of sheer exhaustion. I just wanted to build something, anything, a car maybe? Or a giant German Christmas-candle pyramid? I needed to use my hands. The work of the mind is exhausting (or can be) but the exhaustion of manual labour brings a rest that is rare and reassuring. I have found that during the periods in my life in which I have had to work predominantly with my mind things have gradually lost their proper perspective. Painting, decorating, building, gardening, even housework, leaven the soul. I needed to build something but I didn't realise then that this urge to build would ultimately spend itself in a garden.

I have always loved being outside; I love the sky, the rich and crumbly soil, all that grows, romps and flies about – in short, the full panoply of peace that is available to us on our doorstep. This is what I go back to and touch every time I have to. This garden started in truth because I had to make that journey back outside. I have to make it now. I have to make it repeatedly. I make it several times a day.

When someone dies it can feel, oddly, like a triumphant failure; with both words carrying their true meaning, right up to the point of the closed door. There is triumph in the journey and yet there is the sense of a harvest that will never again be gathered, a crop that has been lost for good. No more seeds, no more plants, no more green shoots. True failure. The failure a farmer might have felt when he looked towards a cold winter with nothing in the barn.

Growing away from danger

The death of my parents wasn't my first taste of failure or, for that matter, shame. In fact, at some level, I had spent my life growing away from danger. I am blessed in that I have always been able to dazzle, at least to a point, if I need to. It takes effort, it takes anxiety, it has a cost: but I can do it. I dazzled my way into Cambridge, into my father's affections (though, as it turns out, I didn't really need to) and into a myriad of different career paths; each abandoned just as it became outwardly successful. This ability to dazzle is useful, it is a blessing of sorts, but in a very important way it is not sufficient. It can leave you very, very empty.

Cambridge was a surprise. I went to a posh boarding school, but one that at the time had a pretty appalling academic record. For most of my childhood, my academic record was pretty appalling too. I have a form of dyslexia that doesn't affect my ability to read but makes spelling, other than phonetically, hard. I think it also hinders my ability to pick up foreign languages. I suspect all this was doubled up and pressed down by a fair amount of attention deficit disorder; leg tapping, fidgeting, twitching, grunting, jumper and shirt sucking and blinking oddly (and with an unnerving intensity), which is something of a family trait.

Still, it was an outwardly defiant and inwardly nervous little boy who trundled around in charcoal grey shorts and an Aertex shirt at prep school. As my brother once said, I appeared to be 'full of twitch and scratch'. I was also prone to bouts of extreme enthusiasm, which I think others found challenging. Taken together, all of this rather hindered my ability to rise within the relatively old-fashioned hatcheries in which I found myself, riddled as they were by a certain amount of natural schoolboy competitiveness. The fact that I was also terrible at sport and recoiled from any organised collective activity, except from boisterous hymn singing, didn't help either.

From about the age of fifteen, I decided I wanted to be a writer and proceeded to write two hideous novels. I haven't looked at them for twenty years but I know more or less what they contain: in retrospect, quite an accurate picture of my future angst; their heroes were out of control. On the upside, I shed a measure of the twitch and scratch as I went on up through the schooling system but in other respects things didn't change much until I was in the sixth form at my senior school.

My father never lost confidence in me or my academic ability. It was during a drive with him, beside Loch Muick in Scotland, that I decided I wanted to go to Cambridge to study theology. When I announced this to my school they said that my prospects were poor and, in fact, they initially refused to

18

support my application. If they did, they argued, when I ultimately failed Cambridge would not take seriously the next, worthier candidate they supported. This line of argument strengthened my resolve, and my father, for his part, was incandescent with fury. He wrote for newspapers quite frequently and, in a rage, he threatened to expose the school for its uselessness in the national press and somehow, together, we made them fold.

In the end, the school supported my application. I worked like anything and got the grades Cambridge required: straight As. I still remember with crystal clarity the bright sunny morning when my grades arrived in an envelope from the examination board. I remember stealing myself away to open the envelope and I remember telling my father, bursting with excitement, as I found him by the magnolia trees he had planted down one side of the house. They were in flower, he was in flower, I was in flower. It was a moment of sheer ecstasy and we shared the ecstasy in completely equal measure.

When I eventually went to Cambridge I discovered that the university had so few applicants from the school I had attended that any failure on my part as a supported applicant would have meant absolutely nothing to them. They had barely heard of the place. I also think my experience shows that some children find their academic feet late.

At Cambridge, things started to unravel, and fast. I had climbed my first summit in life and found it didn't hold the answers I craved. I quested for peace, for fulfilment and for belonging, and my quest took me to some rather unpleasant places. Off the rails would be an understatement; my journey took me through narcotics, unrequited love and misplaced desire. It took me through enough booze to sink a battleship and eventually to a magistrates' court on the Horseferry Road in London. Before my turn in front of the beak there was a lady of the night being sentenced for plying her trade. The law forced the judge to ask her how she would earn the money to pay her fine. The magistrate's face was grizzled and embarrassed. She answered simply: 'How do you think?' I stared into a misery far greater than my own and I resolved to do something. Ground zero.

Back from the edge

Luckily, I had a patient and kind tutor at Cambridge who went out of his way to gently tease me back to my studies, and to some sort of normal approach to life. He stood to gain nothing from his efforts (and in fact shouldered a fair amount of professional risk simply by trying to help me), so I was and am grateful. A number of other things changed at this time and the one I am happy to have with me each day as I wake up now is my wife. A girl with bright blue eyes bumped into my life and brought in her wake a tide of good sense.

More than this, she backed me despite my deeply unorthodox upbringing. She saw me as worth rescuing. At the time, she felt like she had spent all the available capital she had with her parents, and she stood against much of the rest of her family, but she agreed to marry me. The stable I came from, with my father's less than conventional approach to marriage and family life, together with my own recent misadventures, must have terrified her parents. Like my father and my tutor, she has never lost confidence in me.

So happily, very happily, I found a little square of land that I could stand on. Since then I have been growing away from danger. Sometimes you are taken to the edge. The edge can be an exhilarating and painful place. It can be genuinely dangerous too. I believe we can be called back from the edge because, in the end, any time on the edge that is unnecessary is selfish time. I was lucky to be called back by a girl with bright blue eyes. She has taught me a lot.

People battle different adversaries, but the one that has taken me to the edge more frequently than not is anxiety. I don't mean worry, which is merely a sort of symptom that can be ignored, but the chemical and biological consequence of trying to live a normal life when your biochemistry is behaving as if you are in the throes of mortal combat with a lion. For periods, mercifully short and now distant, it forced me into my bed, where I spent long stretches of unpleasant time in a sort of trippy headspace and with a metallic taste in my mouth. The worst period was not when my father died, but when he was very, very ill.

During his illness my world had shaken and heaved and wrenched itself from its sprockets. And as I fought it, it wrenched and heaved more. I thought I might be going mad. There was nothing but shifting; a long haul through existential quicksand. At its worst, you simply can't do anything; gradually I learnt to switch on a sort of autopilot that enabled me to function and accomplish tasks in a way that outwardly appeared normal, though inwardly I was in a sort of frozen stall. I did this for my son. He was a toddler. I could still enjoy building things with him.

When my father was so ill he could only communicate by looking at letters on a board I told him what I was going through. This may sound odd, but it is a mark of his gargantuan strength and commitment to truth that I knew I could share it with him, notwithstanding his ill health, without leaving him in the conventional sense 'worried'. Though he had never spoken of it before, letter-by-letter he spelt out his own experience. His thirties had been filled with exactly the same thing. No one who knew him could possibly have guessed. He seemed never to flinch, even when in grave physical danger. He had clearly learnt to turn on the autopilot too.

In my early teens my father let me go harrowing with the small tractor. A harrow is like a giant piece of chainmail with spikes hanging down that is dragged across pasture. Its purpose is to scarify; to scratch out dead grass and moss and to lacerate the surface of the soil at the same time. I loved this. I loved the fact that something other than me was pulling a great weight of metal across the landscape, seemingly effortlessly.

Extreme or otherwise, anxiety has always left me feeling that I am pulling a great harrow through pasture, with each hair on my head connected to the chainmail. Torrid step by torrid step. Each jot and tittle in the land pulsating along the thread that is connected to my head. But this is a lie. The truth always sets you free. What is needed is to take a sharp blade and ruthlessly cut the hair and the harrow off. Prune away the branches as you would dead wood from a tree. None of us are bound to a harrow. Whatever your brain chemistry happens to be doing, Michel de Montaigne's words remain mercifully true: 'My life has been full of terrible misfortunes, most of which never happened.'

Starting to see a garden

My strongest advice to anyone designing a new garden, or improving an existing one, is to look hard at the topography of the ground that is already there. This is absolutely where I started with this garden. To start to see the future garden you have to acclimatise yourself thoroughly to the current one. I have walked every inch of this garden many, many times. I have lain down flat on the grass and crawled around to get a better perspective on something. I have climbed ladders to get a different view and spent hours looking at the garden from the top floor of the house and thinking with my eyes. I have thoroughly stalked every inch of this garden.

When we arrived I knew that below the elm hedge I had a largely blank canvas. To me this was a great joy. In part this was pride (which is always vain and stupid) but I think in larger part it was the urgent need I had to create, to spend frustration and wrap it into purpose. Only something new would do. Of course, no blank canvas is truly blank. There exists already the natural topography, the soil you must learn, and the arc of the sun that you must observe through the seasons.

In our first winter, I was out planning and digging; digging and planning. This winter, three years on, I have been too. Every winter I think there may be less digging to do, but there never is. When you are building a new garden jobs must be done in a seasonal order. Beds have to be prepared in the winter, so they can be planted in the spring.

For better or worse, my approach to garden design is in some ways the opposite to everyone else's. I don't start with what the client (in this case, me) wants; neither do I start in a room with tracing paper and coloured pencils, or with a preordained sense of the style wished for. I start at the other end. I start with what the garden wants.

I have a sense, rather like Plato's world of ideas, that the ideal garden for any plot already in some way exists and my job is merely to find it. I use the existing topography, the soil and the arc of the sun, and I then set about trying to discover the garden as if it were already there. I have found that getting to the bottom of each garden room has felt more like a process of discovery than something I have pushed out through mental effort. My mind seems to hover over the space and, if I watch for long enough, I start to see it. Sometimes I can go for ages and see nothing; other times discoveries come thick and fast.

While this may all sound highfaluting, when you stop and think about the high degree to which gardens are governed by their unique topography, weather, microclimates, soil and share of light, it makes quite a lot of sense as a practical notion. All the decisions I have made because I had a preconceived idea about something I 'wanted' have seemed to me later to be wrong. All the things I have discovered by simply being in the garden and somehow seeing them have seemed to me later to be right.

I took the same approach in our tiny London garden. I just spent time in it and as I did it grew around me in my mind. The process was the same, but in some ways a little easier. It was easier to ensure succession in the beds and easier to ensure sufficient mass to feel the garden was set apart from the city. On the other hand, it was less forgiving and small errors had a greater impact. Despite being no more than twenty-six feet by twenty-six feet, it felt like an audacious garden to me at the time, packed as it was with twelve climbing roses, three flowering trees, plenty of evergreen, a dedicated herb garden and an array of spring tulips better in some ways than the one I have now. The only downside to our new garden was having to say goodbye to our old one; it is always hard saying goodbye to an old friend.

Placing the emphasis on being in the garden is a simpler and easier approach for an ordinary person who wants to improve their garden than tracing paper and coloured pencils. There is nothing wrong with making sketches, and they become necessary when you are trying to share your vision with someone else (I certainly have made a great number building our garden here), but there is no substitute for pacing your garden.

In some senses, I view our house as merely the most convenient way for me to be able to actually live in my garden. I felt the same in London. It is definitely not the other way around. It is all about being. Being in the garden.

Learning your eard

The Saxons had a relationship with the *eard*, literally the soil on which we all walk, that reached out beyond, and in some senses wrapped up, all their other relationships. The *eard* is why they fought. The maintenance and protection of the *eard* was why they accepted social hierarchy. The *eard* itself reached through time too, providing a mysterious shared inheritance. Culture, politics and nation stood on, and emerged from, our rich and crumbly English soil. They loved *engel lond*, they loved it because it was the place where the *eard* could be found.

Once you have learnt a garden above ground, you must begin to learn what it's like below ground too; you must thoroughly learn your *eard*. The great advantage of the smaller garden we had in London was that this was the job, almost, of an afternoon. I simply created the soil conditions I wanted.

But here the scale of the job (learning seven acres) required a new level of commitment; particularly a commitment to digging.

Building this garden has been a gut-wrenching attempt to recreate something of Eden in north Essex. An enterprise that has strained my sinews, my creative will and my relationships with those I love. I can't accurately explain where this level of commitment comes from, or why it is there. Often it has been almost all-consuming. I wake up with the garden in my thoughts more often than not. I dream about it and I regularly hit hypoglycaemic walls cultivating it. But for the first year this was all largely related, in one way or another, to digging.

Digging mostly happens in the winter. When I was younger I used to fish on the lake at home with a float. I would spend twelve-hour stretches watching the little float bobbing up and down on the surface of the water waiting for a 'big one'. In those days, when I went to bed, I would fall asleep and see the float still bobbing up and down in my mind, and so it is after a day's solid digging; as I go to sleep I can see the soil and I can see the rhythm of the spade working.

Other than the cost of plants, and the patience imposed by the seasons, the only thing that stands between me and what I hope to create is the speed at which I can dig. When I start to dig I reckon I can either excavate and shift a good ton of soil a day – or simply shift (with no excavation) three tons. This assumes in both cases the day is filled with other ordinary tasks such as school runs, feeding animals, talking to my family, etc. I estimate that the digging burns as many, if not more than, 2,000 calories. The soil can feed us, but it can also keep us fit. Neither is it just about the means of production; it is about the sheer thrill of it. We might one day travel to another galaxy, or make quantum computers that will answer our questions before we ask them, and all this is good, but if we anaesthetise ourselves from the thrill of production, for all our cleverness, we will risk leaving a part of ourselves forever behind.

You have to develop the ability to look at your soil with unblinking eyes, to really learn it. Now, for example, I know where, a hundred years ago, the animals were stabled. I know this because of the texture of the soil and because of the extravagance of the plants that grow within it. This is why two beds in the rose garden grow plants that rush beyond their peers next door. I know where the underground gullies run, and more importantly where they do not. These are places of quagmire in winter. I know where the topsoil is deepest and where the clay sits just under the top layer of grass. I know where mounds are true mounds, as opposed to the spoil from some long-forgotten project. Soil simply has to be learnt and, in my case to begin with, this meant an awful lot of digging. Despite three years of digging and mulching our garden remains in its extreme infancy, embryonic really.

Our soil is clay, which is somewhere between a mixed blessing and a lot of hard work. On the upside clay is packed with nutrients. However, unless radical steps are taken this is often of limited benefit to the roots of a plant because in its raw state it is not easily workable for them. The nutrients remain locked within an impermeable clay barrier. There are some exceptions; roses, lilacs, honeysuckle and poppies, for example, all seem to like my clay.

To make the best of the nutrients locked within a clay soil you need to break it up (lighten it) and the only feasible way of doing this on scale is to add masses of organic matter, either through digging it in or through mulching heavily and letting the worms do the work. When I started this garden I

31

relied on the age-old practice of 'double digging' every bed, but now I have learnt to dig less and mulch more; because worms (and if you mulch heavily and garden organically you will have plenty of worms) leaven the soil without destroying its structure. They rise up to the organic matter and then draw it back down deep into the soil. It is most considerate of them!

In terms of what to mulch with, compost, leafmould or well-rotted straw and animal wallop will do. Preferably all three; they all bring something different to the party. Leafmould is the best for improving soil structure but doesn't deliver any nutritional benefit, whereas both compost and wallop will feed soil and improve its structure. Wallop produced by birds, known as guano, holds the most nutrients, but all wallop, so long as it is well rotted, is a good thing. Adding horticultural grit to soil is great, but expensive. It is rarely practical to use sand, because in most cases it would require far too much to have the desired effect. In my first winter, however, I poured vast quantities of sand into what was meant to become a vegetable patch. I did so before being certain of its position and I am sad to report I now have a very well-drained patch of meadow.

By a similar token, those people who have light, free-draining soil (such as in Hampshire) will need to make it denser so it retains water and nutrients. The same medicine can be prescribed: add as much organic matter as you can, but don't trouble to add any grit or sand. At the end of our first growing season I made a large investment in this garden's bank account. A new friend down the valley keeps horses and had a massive pile of muck in the corner of a paddock. I asked him if I could have the best bits and he not only let me, he lent me his trailer. I shifted tons, all of which has wound its merry way into the soil of the rose garden.

Building a new garden makes you greedy for organic matter, and you need to find a ready supply nearby. Gardening friends may be reticent to share with you what they do for fear of their own supply drying up. Some people swear by spent mushroom compost so, if you have a local mushroom farm, that is another option. Friends here keep bags and a shovel in their cars so they can make the most of the horse wallop they find on the country lanes round about. If I had a smaller garden I would do the same. I love the smell of horse wallop. It is a clean, even an honest smell.

Here, I have a combined approach. I keep chickens so all of their wallop goes in. One way or another we also produce a fair amount of kitchen waste (about a large bin-full a week) so that goes in. Windfall, grass cuttings, small woody cuttings and some leaves go in (such as chestnut leaves, because they take too long to break down into leafmould). All the by-product from my propagating and potting mixtures go in. One way or another, therefore, we produce a fair amount of well-rotted organic matter ourselves.

It is important your mixture rots down properly and swiftly. You can speed this up by adding an activator. Pee is a good activator and I encourage members of the family to add to the compost heaps as they pass. The children rather took to this and decided to keep a potty next to the main heap. With a garden this size I have learnt that it pays to have composting stations in various parts of the garden. However well-intentioned you are, the convenience of this approach means more stuff overall finds its way into the composting system. Finally, it is best to ensure your compost heap sits on soil rather than hardstanding because it will benefit from the microbes and worms below it. Turning heaps regularly with a fork speeds things up, too. While all this means work, it is a question of improving your *eard*. When your soil becomes what gardeners call friable (that is dark, crumbly and gorgeous to touch and handle) it will cause you great pleasure and immeasurably improve the quality of the plants you grow.

Standing against the season

For me it was a great advantage that we arrived in the winter. Bleakest midwinter, when the trees stand stark and close against the skyline, is quite simply the very best time to assess a garden's basic structure; its trees, hedges, paths and other hard landscaping. But in addition to this, it is the time to establish what, if any, evergreen there is. It was always important to me that, when I had a garden, it would stand against the privations of winter.

In the same way that a magician has a box of tricks, a gardener can have an array of flowers to last all winter long. You can (and I do) grow Christmas box and winter-flowering clematis. Or snowdrops with clumps of *Iris reticulata*. Or burnished stands of dogwood and willow. And so the list goes on. But this is not what I mean by a garden that stands strongly against the season. During the winter, when the uncontrollable fullness of summer is past, and no amount of flowering clematis will bring it back, it is so often the shapes provided by evergreen that are left to please the eye.

This is where the English gardener's use of box, yew and holly reaches a pinnacle of horticultural mastery; but growing a box ball in the middle of a flowerbed will often do the trick, and give a whole bed a winter presence. Delivering this effect in London was easy (and relied heavily on a single neatly trained silver tassel bush, which delighted us all winter long with its elegant catkins and evergreen foliage). Now, with more room, I have a far wider palette. Using yew, box, holly and even bay I have written some winter substance into both the rose garden and the home garden. It is slight at the moment, but with every year it will stand more firmly against the season.

The palette available is in fact vast; from winter-flowering viburnum through spring-flowering laurel to an Italian cypress tree (quite a tricky customer in the garden as opposed to on a Tuscan hillside) or, for that matter, all the conifers. I find it pleasing to have a variety of foliage types, but ensuring a good splash of green all through the winter is surprisingly easy. I try to create a pattern that repeats throughout the home garden and rose garden, in all their nooks and crannies.

The meadow, with its vast central plateau like the nave of a great cathedral, can look bleak and barren under a weak winter sun, contrasting with and magnifying the warm heart of the rest of the garden. I have considered providing an evergreen element to the avenue (staggered topiary, for example) but I am not sure I want to lose the bleakness yet or remove the drama of the dichotomy. The bleakness there underlines the warmth here. Being on the right side of a pane of glass in a rainstorm only works because there is such a thing as the wrong side. Still, at the garden's core, I am aiming to use evergreen in such a way that it provides the visual equivalent of a rhyme and cadence that speaks of comfort; of all the ingenious ways in which man has learnt to survive the privations of winter.

This rhyme and cadence can be found beyond planting, of course. I see it woven into topography. It is a myth that East Anglia is flat. Parts of Norfolk and mid Suffolk are flat, the fens are clearly flat, but the Stour and Colne rivers run along valleys ground out at the end of the last ice age (the glaciers more or less reached here before retreating) and they left behind them, in addition to the charming mix of gravel, flint and Norwegian clay that I have to contend with on a daily basis, the delightfully undulating countryside of the Essex–Suffolk border beloved of both Constable and Gainsborough. These very undulations stand against the season. They are a topographical citadel; they are the warm embrace of a pleasant *eard*.

Now, three years into building this garden and at the end of the winter, as I walk out along main avenue, which acts as a yardarm from which the weak winter sun withers, my heart lifts and I long for the tall grasses that will provide maze-like structure all summer long. But I know that by the end of the summer I will long for the clean, clipped expanse that emerges after the annual mow, like a room that has been recently swept. In each season, there is a majesty to the view, and to the progression of the avenue, and to the eventual reveal of the reservoir further up the valley (which emerges about two-thirds down), and to the altar-like cairn where the land falls into the sky, and all this taken together just seems to sing. I haven't yet grown tired of it. It has not been worn down through familiarity. Even now, three years in, the garden as a whole stands squarely against privation. It warms me in a way that the superior heat, bustle and mass of a city never could.

Making my escape

I had wanted a change. I wanted what I had always wanted – a life and career in the country – but I wasn't being entirely honest with myself (or anyone else), least of all my wife Sybilla.

Within a week or so of our first visit to Peverels we had, to our surprise, agreed a price with the vendors. As we weighed up our chances of extracting a sufficiently large mortgage from the bank, itself a hair-raising process, the whole question of my work came up. For Sybilla, the one thing that would have ruled out buying Peverels would have been if it had endangered my work. I was smooth-talking her with plenty of discussion about how easy it would be for me to commute daily to London on the train, and how incredible it was that so many trains went daily from Marks Tey. I was seeking to reassure her that my comfortable,

London-orientated trajectory was not in danger; she had good reason to be concerned. I had form.

During our twelve years in London I set up three entirely different businesses; the first in public relations, the second a novel approach to leasing office space and, finally, providing advice to industry. In each case, I taught myself something completely new and launched myself into the blue yonder. In each case, my plan was to get rich enough, quickly enough, to promptly escape to the country with enough money stored up to be able to garden or farm. In my mind, this would somehow tie up two apparently opposing objectives; I would be able to provide my family with something similar to the rewards that can accrue from a London career while also living as far away from London as practically possible. With the benefit of hindsight I can see that this plan, while possibly noble in some regards, was also riddled with a youthful optimism bordering on complete foolishness. I was trying to set myself up in one type of life only so I could then abandon it.

Each of the businesses I set up was profitable enough to pay me a decent salary within the first six months, and yet each was abandoned just when it was on the verge of becoming publicly successful. I can now see why this happened. In each case, I had huge dreams and visions. In each case, these dreams and visions collided with reality and, as that happened, the prospect of my making 'enough' money (a silly amount) to retire to the country got pushed further and further away, until it was so far away I lost hope. This caused me to give up and try something else that might generate more cash, more quickly. A fool's progress.

This was all understandably very trying for Sybilla, and even quite confusing for me. I still feel guilty about putting her through it. The truth is, none of the jobs I did reached that deeper part of my soul, because they were all a means to an end, and the end kept trotting off into the impossibly far-off distance. However, the great thing about Peverels, as I explained to Sybilla, was that I could commute and therefore keep, and even grow, my latest business.

Looking back, I can see there was a dishonesty of sorts in my position, but at the time it was felt rather than articulated. I really did intend to commute from Peverels, and I really did intend to grow my business. I bought the house thinking that if this ever changed, it would at least be with Sybilla's agreement. But at a very deep level I also bought it knowing that in some way I hadn't anticipated our plans were unrealistic. I knew somehow that however carefully we laid our plans, reality was on its way to dislodge them. In any case, the urgent need to escape the close air of London, on almost any terms, was now so pressing I couldn't hold it off for a moment longer than necessary.

With my father gone, and the farm my family had lived on gone, I couldn't bear interminable weekends stuck in London with no escape other than the fabricated countryside of a city park, which served only to remind me even more pressingly of what I didn't have. Now, when I visit a city, the parks are my favourite places; but then, they just reminded me that I was failing to live the life I wanted; failing miserably. Grey slanting rain with no roaring hearth. Miserable.

For me entering a big city has always felt a little like walking into the white noise of an untuned TV screen; it constantly unsettles me, and yet I have had to live in them for long tranches of my life. Cities have always felt like adult boarding school; when I have to sleep in them I see only sad separation, never togetherness. I feel disjointed. I was desperate to get out and get home. I longed for the crumbly earth. I knew once I was out, I could come back to the city and enjoy the best it had to offer; daytime visits only, safe in the knowledge a bed was waiting for me somewhere else; sunk deep within the green folds of England's pleasant *eard*. My father once told me that cities were places to win prizes, but not places to live. People bemoan a long commute but I would take it over an urban weekend without hesitation.

So, I felt like a prisoner planning his escape. It may sound like a very ungrateful way to talk about living in one of the greatest cities in the world, and it probably is. Dr Johnson's entreaty that 'when a man is tired of London, he is tired of life' passed frequently through my mind. But for me that wasn't the point, and, in any case, I knew that I was far from tired of life. But as long as we were pavement-bound I felt caged.

As Sybilla and I prepared to move up to Peverels we were excited and anxious. At about this time I had received a small cheque from my grandmother. It was enough money to have made a meaningful contribution, for example, to taking the family away on holiday for a week. But I decided that I wanted to buy something that I could keep, to remind me of Granny. She was the only one of my grandparents I had known. A friend pointed out to me that there was an East Anglian sale coming up at Bonhams and suggested that I should look to see if I could find anything for our new house. I was dubious; the amount of money in question didn't seem like enough to buy fine art, but he said it was an 'affordable' sale so I had a flick through the catalogue anyway.

I found a painting of a boat straining on a very rough sea just off the coast of Ipswich. It was by a local artist and the painting had a lighthouse in the foreground with a cross on top. It was within budget, so I called Sybilla and we agreed a not-very-high upper limit to the amount that we would be prepared to pay for it. It was a quiet room. We bid for it and, amazingly, we got it. As I took the painting home, a part of my mind hovered over that rough North Sea. I wondered if our move to the country might be choppy in some way not yet foreseen. I also thought of the solidness of the lighthouse, which put my mind at ease.

A staggered arrival

Our discussions with the bank concluded positively and we bought the house on 8 August 2013. The night before we completed I couldn't sleep a wink. We were finally leaving London, though frustratingly not immediately. It was to be a staggered escape. I remember standing under the huge chestnut at Peverels hearing, on my mobile phone, that both sets of papers had been signed and the keys could be handed over. I feel a tingle at the back of my neck still as I write these words. We were in, sort of. We wouldn't be able to move in full-time until December. But December wasn't so far away. I knew that I couldn't shout and scream with joy because David, one part of the David and Mette team who had stewarded this place for the last twenty years, was standing next to me and for him this must have been a profound moment. I shook his hand, I thanked him and inwardly I promised him we wouldn't let him down – we would try to be good stewards of Peverels too.

The interregnum between when we bought Peverels in August and when we moved into it properly in December was largely down to work. We had two whole weeks here over the summer and then we shuttled up at weekends but spent weekdays in London until 13 December. Two days before my son's seventh birthday, under the cover of a blanket of sparkling ice, we moved in for good. Those first few months when we were here only at weekends were thrilling.

On the other side of the equation were the stacks of boxes left half unpacked and the painful trips back to London on a Sunday evening that autumn and winter. Quite apart from the fact that travelling anywhere with small children requires stopping frequently to change nappies, administer bottles or mop up sick, I found the moment when Canary Wharf loomed into view on the M11, winking menacingly from its pinnacle, particularly depressing. It would bring a sinking feeling as I girded myself for yet another week in London when my mind and heart were elsewhere, walking the house and garden at Peverels.

Sunday-afternoon blues were something I knew well enough from my childhood, being part of a generation who were sent off to boarding school aged seven. A mixture of anxiety, a sort of undirected longing together with excitement (and that metallic taste in the mouth) always accompanied the two-hour drive back to school after a weekend at home. Today, Sunday afternoons bring with them a slight momentary pang, rather like a memory echo. Now that we are settled in our home, and I don't have to leave for either school or London, Sunday afternoons also bring with them a rill of happy excitement. I acknowledge inwardly that I will be in the same place the following morning and a cool wave of satisfied relief washes over me. Every Sunday.

Despite the newfound joy of a Sunday afternoon, we had our concerns even after our arrival in December. Our first experience of Peverels had been not being able to find it. Even with satnav and my rather dubious orienteering skills we just somehow couldn't get there. Peverels is nestled in an impenetrable crisscross of ancient Iron Age lanes. The largest conurbation to the east is Colchester, which historically together with its neighbouring ports (Brightlingsea, Harwich, Felixstowe) created a hub of economic activity that travelled inland, but only to a point, because it was caught by the A12 (itself an ancient byway) and funnelled towards London. To the west, the biggest city is Cambridge, but that would have been a day's ride away. Similarly the largest town to the north, Bury St Edmunds, is another day's ride. In short, Peverels, then as now, is in a sort of forgotten pocket of country that no one goes through unless they happen to be actually going to it. I would call it rural. Some would call it isolated. In either case, it is a long way from the frappuccinos of Parsons Green in Fulham.

I knew the adjustment to rural living would be far harder for Sybilla to make with three children in tow than for me. I don't mind if I go for days without seeing people (other than family). But for Sybilla, everything in London had been set up, everything worked. I hoped that the first few months, during which we suffered a dual country and city life, might help soften the blow.

On the other hand, Sybilla too had tired of being shouted at in our tiny kitchen in London and had longed for a garden into which she could turf the kids. We had looked and looked but couldn't find anything that fitted what we wanted. We both wanted a truly rural idyll, which is hard to find in the south of England. In a very peculiar turn of events, one morning while I fruitlessly searched on the computer in the kitchen in London, over the din being created by the kids, Sybilla joked: 'Isn't there a village called Great Shouting? That's the place for us.'

There was no village called Great Shouting but I remembered there was one called Great Yeldham in north Essex, so given that my search to the west of London had been completely hopeless (everything was too expensive), I idly plugged Great Yeldham into Rightmove. That act, followed by a few circuitous twists and turns, ended in our finding and buying Peverels.

Even though Sybilla was nervous about leaving her comfortable, organised and well provisioned life in London, together with her network of supportive friends (many of whom also had small children), for the uncertainties of a new life in a small farmhouse five hundred yards down a track, in an area where we hardly knew anyone, we both knew, deep down, it was time. Our eldest (at the time six) was bouncing off the walls and his two sisters (three and two) weren't far behind.

One other issue loomed into view during this period. Sybilla would need to get a driving licence. In London she hadn't needed one and was too busy for the whole kerfuffle of lessons anyway. Now, however, she would urgently need one. While we were aware of this, we didn't think too much about it. Our plan was that to begin with I would do all the driving (whether children, friends or food) into and out of the farmhouse, but Sybilla would start driving lessons on 1 January.

We never stopped to consider, before making this relatively major financial and lifestyle commitment, what life at Peverels would be like if Sybilla, for some reason, wouldn't be able to drive. Or whether we could even stay there. We just weren't practical enough for that sort of thought process and, anyway, far too distracted by the excitement of moving into a new home. Also, we are by nature optimists. Everything was set. Sybilla would start her driving lessons in the New Year and pass her test shortly thereafter. We thought no more of it.

One more very important thing happened that first winter. We discovered, to our surprise but delight, that Sybilla was pregnant with our fourth child. We joked about her being pregnant while learning to drive and whether this would cause undue stress for whoever the instructor happened to be. It all just seemed funny.

What wasn't funny was that my mother, albeit slowly, now seemed to be entering her final chapter. It had become clear it was a question of when, not if. As we told her about Sybilla's pregnancy I could see that she was determined to remain alive until the baby arrived. My mother was tough and I knew that this would become her final milestone. Whichever way you looked at it, change of one sort or another was now coming at us thick and fast.

Winter's close in that first year found us in a dreamy (if extremely rural) house slap-bang in the middle of undulating English countryside. We had not only bought the house, we had finally managed fully to move into it. Outside was a vast empty garden waiting for my attention. Inside was a list of jobs as long as my arm. Moving with three children under six was tiring but desperately exciting. I had vastly expansive dreams for our life together here and for the garden. I couldn't wait to sit on a warm evening on the wall with my son and look nonchalantly at the pond, which by the time things warmed up, would have ducks on it. I couldn't wait to enjoy East Anglian sunsets together. Every day I walked the garden, thinking, looking, trying to see what was truly there. Long list after long list was drawn up and I scrabbled to prioritise which jobs should come first. During that first winter I had spent a morning digging two new flowerbeds under the wall by the magnolia tree. In went some nuclear-coloured pansies from the local nursery. Sybilla seemed underwhelmed as I forced her out into the cold to look. But it was a start.

We also found ourselves with empty address books – other than old family friends on my side, we didn't know a single person our own age in the area. We had found new schools for our children and we were watching the kids like hawks to see if they were happy and settling in. This anxiety will be immediately recognisable to any parent in the country who has packed their little bundle off to a new school for the first time.

Still, everything was good, everything was poised, everything was new. It is not so often, after all, that you get to change everything in your life, and there is something reenergising about it. The kids were all very excited and so were we. I felt like a champion at the end of a very long marathon.

My soil

We can't escape the soil into which we are planted. The ground determines what will grow and, moreover, how it will grow. But that isn't the end of the matter. Improvements can be made. All good work takes time. Sometimes blood, sweat and tears. Maybe even treasure. People don't realise what champions they are when they start to dig, inside or out.

Digging is best done in winter when the ground is neither frozen nor waterlogged. It is when the fullness and busy distraction of summer has melted away, and all that is left is the stark earth; that is when you can see what you are doing. I think this is why we are sometimes taken to edges; and winter is the garden's edge. With enough moisture and enough cold (but not too much of either) the ground here yields to me and can be cut into like a cake. I take off sods of turf and either stack them grass side to grass side so that the following autumn I can take the valuable topsoil back and return it to the garden, or play with the children at making mud cottages and glance back at the house, warm electric lights on and smoke rising from the chimney.

Until a hundred years ago people across the Celtic fringe, from Cornwall to the Orkneys, lived in mud houses. Winter makes me grateful for the pre-Elizabethan beam, as thick as a bull's neck, which hangs over the staircase, as if guarding the place where we go to sleep. It makes me grateful that I live in a place that has, relatively speaking, been rich throughout recorded history. This soil was known to be rich before the Roman invasion. It is why they came.

The Trinovantes who lived here first, when the place became a place, and before England had happened, were wealthy, highly civilised, trading people. Their capital was Colchester. You can still see an ancient Roman wall that seems to run for ever, beyond time itself, and was built to protect Romano-British wealth. It also protects an old meadow below the castle where wool traders would stretch out their damp fleece on tenterhooks to wait for it to dry. Only when it was dry could they assess the value of the wool they had bought. They waited on tenterhooks.

Everything is on tenterhooks in winter, me included. Everything waits for spring and then harvest. Not everything in the garden will make it; as their stomachs empty, and their strength fails, only the fittest songbirds will join in the spring chorus. But this is rich soil and we seek to share the proceeds of its growth, even with the birds. Despite perhaps as many as three millennia of harvests, the soil is still rich. Sometimes the yearning for life to once again flow through the ground is overwhelming. Anyone who has gone digging, inside or outside, knows this feeling.

If the children are with me as I dig they look out for treasure, ever hopeful that I will strike the dull tone of a wooden chest with my spade. I have found no chests but I do find the iron nails that the Elizabethans used to build a shelter around their wool and their harvests and themselves; to protect their treasure. This is hard evidence that progress is possible. That knowledge is where the journey back from the edge always starts.

As I cut and remove turf, the sociable little robin comes looking for treasure too, always. Sometimes the English robin, the one with the redder breast, and sometimes the Scandinavian robin driven south, as were the Danes, by harsh winters and failed harvests. Long after the Romans, the Danes came in waves. Many waves. Their terrifying longboats burnished with shiny metal and carrying their men wound up our river estuaries, including this one. The word berserk is theirs. It is how they fought, in a trance of fury. They were the 'berserkers'. This soil was well within their Danelaw. Their influence still hangs in the air, and in the fair hair and blue eyes of the people.

Rich soil has, after all, always been a prize. I grew up thirty miles north of where we now live, a place where the soil is richer still. It is easier too, with none of the grit left by the retreat, back to the far north, of the great glacier. Hunger can drive man or beast to plunder what they shouldn't. This reminds me that I should teach my children to be grateful for the soil into which they have been planted, protected as it is by diplomats and treaties and fighter jets. Protected, in the end, by rough men who stand ready to do violence on our behalf. This was Orwell's observation, a winter wordsmith if ever there was one. This describes another edge. It is the bleak but reassuring hard edge upon which we all gratefully perch. There is no time for such thoughts in summer when we are all busy with harvest.

Trees

Winter is a good time to think about trees and, for that matter, the other two structural pillars of most gardens: hedges and paths. So much of a garden's soul is won or lost on these three pillars. They are important in all gardens, and perhaps even more so in small ones, where the weight of a wrong decision can seem to sit more heavily within the mass of the overall garden. In London, I could cross my garden in eight short steps but I still poured hours of thought into the three trees it played home to and the emerging hedge of climbing hydrangea that sat on a north-facing wall. The smaller the garden the more important these decisions become. With seven acres I have a larger canvas, but unquestionably a more forgiving one. Paths too must always go somewhere, and preferably come back again. They must have a purpose and reflect a clear intention. Often, they reflect no more than the arbitrary thought that the garden in question ought to have some sort of path. But I didn't start with paths. I started with trees and hedges and paths emerged as a result.

From our bedroom window we can survey the entirety of the garden and, beyond it, the valley basin, and beyond that, the far ridge on the other side of the valley, which is peppered with Lombardy poplars (giving it a Tuscan feel in the summer). So many people live in cities, it feels like an unspeakable privilege to wake up to such a view each morning. In the winter, when the valley is bare, cold and bleak, the rising sun often still throws columns of pink across the garden, like a guilty parent sending an expensive present to their child to substitute for their absence. Winter is about hanging on to what you do have and pegging your hope to the hearth. My trees, new and old, are an important part of this equation.

From my bed I have a clear view of our sixty-foot elm tree in the middle of the great elm hedge. Our part of the country was famous for its elm trees before the dreaded beetle killed them all. Actually, there are still miles and miles of elm hedge because the beetle only attacks once the tree reaches a certain size, so if you keep elm as a hedge, you can keep it indefinitely. But there are some mature-ish specimens that survive, and we are lucky to have four of them. It may be that the beetle simply hasn't found them, or that they have some immunity. No one really knows.

Truly mature elm trees seem to have the habit of a louche aristocrat. If a tree could wear a smoking jacket and ballroom slippers it would be the elm. I sometimes look out the window and imagine what the skyline would have looked like when it was festooned with them. The elm tree has other curiosities. Its leaves are the only ones I can think of that are bevelled at their tips – they curl in disdain as if announcing their superior ancestry. Also, their leaves assume an almost canary-yellow colour in the autumn, painting streaks along our hedges.

They sucker like anything. Within six months of digging the new beds in the rose garden there was a veritable forest springing up from disturbed roots that had travelled as much as thirty feet away from the adjoining hedge. I suppose this proves our elm hedge is old. I am sorry that I will never see a truly mature elm other than in a photograph; I feel the same way about the loss of my father. Things seem to vanish; but not completely. I can see something of him in myself, and certainly in my children, and even if my elm tree one day succumbs to the beetle I will still have the hope of an elm hedge to hold on to. Grief can percolate into everything: into trees, into views, into hedges; into five-minute breaks. It has run through this garden in great torrents. I can do nothing to stop it.

When we arrived I was inordinately proud to suddenly own a large number of very beautiful trees. I was also desperate to get planting; to own not just these, but all the trees I had ever wanted but which had been forbidden to me in London. After all, with seven acres to steward there was no shortage of space in which to site them (or so I felt), and in any case every garden is really a sort of arboretum. I was definitely in a rush, and the old Indian proverb that the best time to plant a tree is twenty years ago went through my mind continually. I wanted Japanese acers to provide streaks of hazardous scarlet that would be visible from the house; lovely crab apples to surprise and delight at bends and turns in what would become paths; tulip trees to flower; ginkgos to beguile; and rare and interesting oddities available along the way. In the first autumn, I got many of the trees on my wish list in, but by no means all.

Gardening can be an inordinately expensive diversion and purchasing trees is at the nose-bleedingly expensive end of the diversion. As a result, I have brought on a great number from seed, even over the last three years, and plenty are now growing away happily in the garden here. While it requires patience, it is in some ways a more rewarding process than a trip to the nursery and in the autumn you can 'have a go' from the seed of a tree you particularly like in a friend's garden. In many cases it is quite easy, as anyone who has potted up an acorn or a horse chestnut knows. Generally, I take a relatively cavalier approach and it seems to work just fine. When I was asked to bring on a batch of perfect oak tree saplings for a garden I would work on at the Chelsea Flower Show, however, I had to inject a little more professionalism. In nine months I brought on a hundred and thirty saplings for an ultimate selection of thirty.

I have learnt there are three things to bear in mind. The first is that some seeds, like ash, require a period of vernalisation. Vernalisation just means the seed requires a cold snap (like the one that it would get during a winter outside) that jolts it into action. You can mimic the cold snap in order to fit in with your own time schedule by placing these seeds wrapped in kitchen paper in the refrigerator, thus mimicking 'winter'. The second is that, as with all plant propagation, the seed rotting is your number-one enemy, so check them while they are in the fridge and ensure the compost you put them in has sharp drainage. Thirdly, fruit trees, for example, will not come true from seed. This is because there is no way of knowing where one half of the parentage comes from (it will come down to the grain of pollen delivered to the flower the previous spring) so what you end up with may not resemble exactly what you propagated from. On the other hand, I find this roulette wheel aspect makes propagating crab apples, for example, more exciting. You might get something worse, but you might get something better. Overall, biology is on your side. Seeds, after all, have a purpose, which is to grow into trees. Your job is to imagine you are the seed and try to provide it with an environment that is as close as possible to the one it would get in nature.

The easiest tree to propagate from cuttings, without doubt, is the willow. I have brought willow on from branches that I have literally torn off the parent plant and plunged into soil. Early on, to shelter the rose garden at no cost, I cut a dozen wands of willow off the coppice by the pond (each was roughly two inches thick and four feet long) and plunged them into the soil at the extremity of the rose garden. I didn't even weed around them (beyond scalping off a spit's worth of turf with a spade) and most took. Willow roots astonishingly easily. In fact, I have used willow to make obelisks for sweet peas before now and had plants growing away happily at the end of the season. I have even heard reports of willow rooting when it has been plunged into the soil upside down. If you plant the smaller ornamental garden willows (such as Kilmarnock), they are grafted onto the root stock of stronger more thuggish ones. These will periodically make a dash for it, sending great stems up from near the ground (below the graft). They must be cut back at the base otherwise they will smother the politer tree you intended to grow.

While a number of the trees I planted in our first winter now thrive, in retrospect I should have applied a diet that consisted of more haste and less speed. While seven acres sounds like an awful lot, actually, given that it falls within a triangle running down a hill, it is less than you think because many trees will grow large and views must be preserved. Over time many of my original plantings have been moved, often to the margins, so that they won't eventually occlude a favourite view. Such are the wages of youthful exuberance. People get squeamish about moving trees (and some, like magnolias, are less inclined to survive upheaval than others), but I always think about the fact that Capability Brown was moving massive trees often very successfully. Many trees will tolerate a carefully orchestrated move, even when quite mature, so on balance I think the emphasis should still be on moving a tree rather than not, particularly in the early years of building a new garden. If necessary, get help and, however young the tree is, always get some sacking under the roots and tie it together to keep the root ball in place.

Some of the trees I planted in the first winter died because in my hurry to have them I planted them in places that were entirely, hopelessly, overoptimistic. A great many trees have adapted in their native habitat to the protection of a superior canopy provided by neighbouring taller trees without which they will languish. Three-quarters of the Japanese acers I planted survive; all the ones that were given a sufficiently protective superior canopy.

When it comes to the technical question of getting a tree into the ground I have three strategies that seem to work for me. I dig generally square holes, not round ones. This means the trees roots can eventually find a corner and break out rather than chasing around an eternal circle and becoming effectively pot-bound. I try to break up as much of the surrounding soil as I can (i.e. the planting hole is as big as possible) but, frankly, this is dependent on the time I can give to each planting, which frequently isn't enough. I don't feed with compost or, if I do, I do so very sparingly, because I don't see the point of providing the tree with false hope and prefer for it to get acclimatised to the soil in which it will grow as soon as possible.

I also stake trees, but I use iron-fencing pins because they provide plenty of give (as opposed to whopping great wooden poles) and the pins are directed with the prevailing wind, so the tree will blow away from the pin as opposed to against it. This is a question of fine balance. If you provide a tree with a crutch, and then at some point in the future kick it away, the tree will stagger (much as a person habituated to using a crutch would). On the other hand, we garden on the side of a west-facing, windy hill. My compromise is the iron-fencing pin and thus far it seems to be a good one. For me, however, the overwhelming argument in its favour is aesthetic. As it rusts to a pleasingly dishevelled, ruddy hue it all but disappears. After a knife and a ball of string I have found iron-fencing pins to be the most useful man-made implement within my garden. They get turned to a great many uses from securing barn doors to supporting plants and being used as giant dibbers; they are readily available in any decent builder's yard.

We lose the odd tree, or parts of a tree, to wind. Leaves on a tree act as sails, which is why autumn storms, before leaf fall, can be so devastating. A tree that is still in leaf (or largely in leaf) and is subject to lashing rain weighing down its boughs, and a punishing wind, is the most in danger of breakage. This is why the very worst storms (as far as trees are concerned) tend to come in October.

I remember clearly the Great Storm of 1987. I was six and, given that it was a weekday, I was in London. The tree outside our house fell and I spent a day climbing on it in my pyjamas. Shortly before the storm my parents' divorce had finally come through. They hadn't lived together really during my lifetime; but I remember aged six walking into the sitting room in London one morning to find my mother with an envelope, weeping. The papers had arrived; it was final; it was the point of capitulation; there was no going back. She put on an incredibly brave face through a flurry of hot tears and despite a completely shattered heart. On the day of the storm I have

61

a very dim memory of her being desperately concerned to hear what had happened in Suffolk. Despite their divorce, despite their no longer living together, she never stopped worrying about my father from that day to his last; her best thoughts were always for him.

I often sit inside by the fire and hear the wind howling outside, nervously thinking of my favourite trees. Wood that does fall is, of course, good news for the log store and I gather it up greedily. In our first winter, we lost a laburnum that was useless, because when it burns it releases noxious gases. A friend told me that an old-fashioned way to parse how well a wood will burn is where its name sits in the alphabet. The lower down the alphabet you go, the less good the wood is for burning. Certainly, apple and ash are the two best woods to burn; they let off a splendid sweet vanilla scent, truly the smell of winter. Chestnut is a poor burning wood, and yet high up the alphabet. But while there are obvious exceptions I have found the alphabet system works more often than not.

Hedges

My father had a special seat fitted to his tractor so that I could join him for hedge cutting. It was small and peculiarly uncomfortable but I loved it. I remember one breakfast he made a tremendous fuss about the new seat that had been fitted; and as soon as his cigar was lit he took me out to inspect it. I remember him slamming it down into position and the noise of its catch as it caught. I remember being excited. My father was a great smoker; at least three cigars and a pipe a day, and much of it I happily imbibed hotboxing in the tractor as he threw a great flail mower across the miles and miles of hedge at home; he liked snuff too and even when I was as young as seven or eight he used to give me small pinches as a treat from time to time. He absolutely loved cutting the hedges. He loved it for its strategic agricultural merit; for its artistry; and for the end result, which he would proudly show off, as the epitome of stewardship in action, to me and anyone else who happened to be ligging around at the time.

I was still bobbing up and down on that seat in my late teens. One conversation that took place while on that seat turned in great detail on which factor principally resulted in our not having an English revolution: was it the visible horror of the French one or the rise of utilitarianism and cheap postage here? All the while, a great head of mechanised steel was tearing through thick Suffolk hedges as he peered through the fug at the line he was creating outside. Occasionally we would hit a rut and I would bounce out of the makeshift chair altogether and onto the tractor's floor. I loved every minute of it and gave the habit up only when physically I could no longer fit in the space allowed without frequently landing on his lap, which he did not enjoy. The empty seat was swiftly taken up by one of my younger sisters. During the period in London when all this had gone and I was suspended in the white noise of the city, I couldn't bear to even think of these memories; they were too painful.

Today, I don't have a flail cutter on the back of a tractor, but I do have plenty of hedgerow and it is a source of both untrammelled joy and effort. I learnt very quickly that the easiest and simplest way to immediately lift the appearance of this garden (or any garden) is to cut the hedges and edge the beds. If you do little else, these two steps will return a crisp and an authoritative feel to a garden overnight.

Each of the last three winters has seen the planting, not just of new trees but new hedges also. I have found the planting of one hedge often calls for the planting of another separate hedge elsewhere to achieve balance; but this only becomes really apparent once the first hedge is in. Even with a master plan to hand, working this process through can be gradual and essentially rationed by the time available in any given season. In my experience, no plan, however carefully formulated, survives contact with the enemy!

The thing I have noticed about master plans (particularly in the context of building a garden) is that they usually buckle when confronted with the messy business of real life. If they are then slavishly adhered to, the end result becomes sanitised and brittle. As you start to lay out a garden, new opportunities emerge that are simply too good to miss and just weren't visible at the outset. I have found again and again that until step two is complete, step three has remained partially obscure. This may of course simply reflect a limitation of mine when it comes to careful foresight and detailed planning (something my family remind me of frequently), and it would make commercial garden design almost unworkable, but I think it may also capture something of the reality of the creative process. Can all painters see the finished canvas in their minds before they start?

The Russians have a military doctrine they call *razvedka boem*. Whereas by tradition we in Britain send out reconnaissance units prior to building a careful plan for battle, the Russians commence battle to test the opponent's strength and then conduct reconnaissance, making adjustments as they go along. This is what I do in the garden (and in life more generally). It is perhaps more expensive in terms of mistakes made, but it feels like a more authentic way of engaging with the complexities of life, even those that concern the planting of hedges. As you can imagine, many of my hedging whips have been moved in year two, and again in year three; it has done them no harm.

The normal way of going about creating a hedge is to buy hedging whips. Whips are hedging plants in their first or second year that are lifted from the nursery field, wrapped in straw or paper and then delivered to your local nursery or front door if you use the internet. A fashionable line of argument at the moment is that it is best to start with whips (as opposed to larger, far more expensive container-grown plants) because being transplanted when young they will more readily adapt to their new environs and within a season or two they will have caught up with the larger container-grown specimens you might otherwise have planted. I think this is true, but only to a point. Firstly, people read from this that the same logic applies to planting trees. It doesn't. It will take a one-foot whip an awful long time to catch up with a fifteen-foot tree that is not pot-bound when planted. So it is with hedges. Responsibly grown large hedging plants can work very well; they are just mind-bogglingly expensive.

Hedging whips are best planted before March, though I have planted them in April when pushed. I find where possible it is best to plant trees in the autumn, because given enough time before the cold really sets in they begin to put roots down and, moreover, this process starts up again at the earliest possible moment in the spring, which taken together means they tend to need less watering the following summer. Often, however, I don't get all my trees planted in the autumn so the ones left over get planted in the spring along with any new hedges that are on the to-do list.

In our first winter, my challenge was simply not having enough daylight hours to shift the turf and dig the new beds, hedges and tree-planting holes that I had prioritised. Sometimes I was tempted to rush, but this is always a mistake. Lots of bamboo canes, lots of string, lots of hosepipe for the curves. Lots of adjustments. There is no other way. Perhaps if I was doing it again I would spend money renting a mini-digger.

Cutting the boundary hedges during our first winter was ecstatically exciting. I knew I was introducing myself to hedges I would get to know intimately, gently and steadily encouraging them to form the shapes I wanted, in order that they could provide a living wall of protection for our family and a tight and elegant frame for our new garden. This sense of shelter spoke particularly to my still raw and untrammelled grief. I needed this sense of making a world apart and the hedges were quite literally our new fortress's walls. Inside them, I was hidden. I felt strongly that they insulated me, not just from the world outside, but from everything else too. I was building a safe enclosed space in which I intended, at some point, slowly to unpick my grief and to see what, if anything, could be done about it.

As a general rule, I have allowed most of the hedges here to get bigger. Shaping hedges, really getting them the way you want, is one of the most rewarding garden jobs. I have made a few mistakes, but of course hedges generally grow back! The exceptions are lavender and leylandii. Neither will break from old wood, so if you cut too hard into the old wood you will get ugly bare patches for which there is no fast remedy. You must always leave some new growth when you cut them, which means that technically they are doomed to always get bigger, even if by an eighth of an inch each year. This is not so relevant to lavender, as the plants don't live much beyond ten or fifteen years, but it might be something to consider when planting leylandii.

People are rude about leylandii, but I think the matter is more finely balanced than suggested by the coverage it generally receives. All too often it is left to get out of control in a suburban setting and a neighbour feels legitimately aggrieved as it gradually squeezes all the light from their garden. But at the same time this illustrates its singular quality: an astonishing (and very useful) rate of growth, particularly, for example, if you need a fast, living, barrier to the wind.

Besides, being a cypress I think leylandii smells lovely and its tiny leaves grouped around spreading stems are delicate and attractive. If cut it will deliver clean and neat lines. It was discovered as a result of a chance cross with a Monterey cypress by Mr Leyland in 1888, since when it has taken, in my opinion, a well-deserved place in the lexicon of British hedging plants, but it must be maintained responsibly.

I have bashed through some hedges to link different parts of the garden and lowered others to open views. Hedges create opportunities for paths that can run along them or dash through them. Cutting observation windows into them is also fun, and opens the view without losing shelter. A hedge is a truly marvellous thing, and will generally shelter an area as much as eight times its own height. Clearly this dynamic is reduced if the area being sheltered is above the hedge on the side of a hill and increased if the inverse is true. I love hedges and they are a principal tool (along with paths and beds) for the gardener to create structure. Can you have too many hedges? I have as much as a mile to cut by hand here each year and sometimes, when the lactic acid starts to bite in my forearms, and my hands are shaking with the exertion, I do wonder; but in general terms the more the merrier.

Hedges are, of course, the single best way in which you can support wildlife. You can judge the age of a hedge by the number of species within it; each species counts for a hundred years. This is generally considered to be a useful guide, even by specialists. The great elm hedge here has at least five species growing in it. It wouldn't surprise me if it were older than five hundred years.

Because most of my mature trees stand within mature hedges they are prone to the vampire advance of ivy. I find it is best to cut a ten-inch gap in the ivy as close to the ground (or to where it meets the tree) as you can and then let it die and wither. If you try to pull lengths of it off you are likely to do no more than damage the tree.

We are fortunate to have a large number of mature trees in the hedges running along our boundaries. It is pleasing to have the odd mature tree breaking the line of a hedge, but not too many, or it quickly becomes a thicket. The mature trees that break through our boundary hedges each have a character of their own. From my study, I can see two cherry trees in our boundary hedge that have grown together as if in a winding embrace; they remind me that here Sybilla and I are building something new.

Paths

After I started out on the process of building the garden, I naturally spoke to friends who were experienced gardeners, more experienced than I am. Other than the importance of planting trees early on (particularly magnolias, if you want them) most discussion was about paths. The one piece of advice that I got several times over was that most people regretted they had not made their paths wider when they laid them. While I think there is a sort of romantic intimacy to a narrow pass, so many people said this I knew it must be true. I designed the paths in the rose garden to allow two people to walk along them comfortably side-by-side. My general rule will be to keep paths generous, but this does mean that for reasons of expense they will remain grass for longer, if not for ever.

I wanted a dainty path to run from the house to the big pear tree, round it and back again. Here I used a bargain basement strategy. Having mowed out the line of the path at the lowest possible setting, I laid some landscape fabric directly on top of the grass and then ran old lengths of wood along its sides. Those were secured in place with hoops of thick wire that I bent for the purpose, each one going more than a foot deep into the soil. I then hefted gravel onto the landscape fabric and raked it flat. It looks great. I built it in a day. On the other hand, if the lawn wasn't as straight as a die, or if you expected any amount of traffic, this method wouldn't work as the path would be liable to float off under the influence of winter rain. My one is fit for purpose.

Bear in mind all wooden structures in a garden will eventually rot and only metal truly stands the test of time, but its longevity comes at a significant price. Also, don't make the mistake of thinking hollow tubes of powder-coated steel (such as are often used for arbours) equals metal. In the end they go the same way as wood too. But all materials will fold and buckle eventually; metal just does it very slowly. The priest who buried my father told me that it had been the first time he had committed someone to the earth in a lead coffin. The only grimly funny moment during the whole bleak January day was when the coffin entered the church and the poor pallbearers had to turn up the aisle. In order to do this they had to negotiate a flimsy wooden internal archway. Crouching down they took half the archway with them and, struggling under the ludicrous weight of the coffin, for one horrible moment it looked as though there was about to be a terrible accident.

My father certainly did all the paths on our farm at home properly, and with all the proper materials. Proper paths require a proper foundation. Usually this is just a question of digging a spit or two down, bashing in some hardcore and then laying your path. On the farm they were either tarmac or concrete; but in a garden setting where the wear and tear doesn't involve vast tractors you can use anything you want as a top dressing. In my case it would always be mellow bricks. The trouble for me is that bricks are surprisingly expensive and the amount of path I need horribly long.

If you merely want to make a path passable in winter there is a sort of compromise: you can leave it grass but lay a narrow strip of something solid down its centre (good enough to walk solo or push a wheelbarrow on). Given the expense, and the huge number of grass paths I would like to make passable in the winter if I could wave my magic wand, this may be my long-term solution. In a secret corner of the garden I am experimenting with a quick and easy way of doing this that involves digging a triangular trench, concrete and some other ingredients, but my results will not be in for a season or two.

Anyone who designs a new garden is likely to have to make a decision, sooner or later, that involves gravel. Often this will arise in the first instance in relation to driveways, paths and areas for passage immediately adjacent to the house. Gravel in gardens is a subject fraught with far more controversy and the need for fine judgement than you might think, and it all comes down to the gauge of the gravel and the depth of the top dressing. Moreover, few people have the moral courage, if presented with a 'mistake', to remove an entire stretch of perfectly good but irritating gravel and replace it with another batch of perfectly good but less irritating gravel, so it is worth giving the matter some thought at the outset.

Even in our first winter it was very obvious that I would have to do something about the drive and that my solution might well involve gravel. The drive runs for several hundred yards, and when we arrived was in effect a dirt track with deep and growing potholes. I looked into tarmac but getting it done would have been extremely expensive. Instead, for less than a quarter of the cost, we opted to improve the hoggin along its length (which involved digging out a weedy strip that had accumulated over decades down the centre) and bashing in hardcore. Then we got tar chippings to glue in the surface, and above this we spread gravel.

The gravel we used is wide (about a one-inch gauge) and matches the gravel round the house. I find people automatically drive more slowly on a gravel surface than on a hard, smooth one, which with children and pets is an advantage. The only downside is that I have to rake it several times a year to maintain a decent top dressing along its length. If I don't keep this top dressing in place, the gravel will spread to the sides and eventually the potholes will re-emerge. Coincidentally, the trick to raking either gravel or soil is to do it unintentionally. That is to say you have to move the rake with abandon over the entire surface area in question. Do not try to individually address hills and valleys.

Now, however, is where the question of gravel depth comes in: if I allow too deep a top dressing by the house, the large-gauge gravel becomes squelchy and difficult to walk across, which is annoying (and this would happen far quicker with a narrower gauge, which all too often feels like walking across a beach). But if the top dressing is too light along the drive I will soon get resurgent potholes. I have to get it just right. I try to keep the dressing of gravel on the drive thick, but around the house shallow, so it barely covers the hoggin below. A narrow-gauge gravel on my hoggin around the house would have to be thick, or else it would melt away into the hoggin. Also, narrow-gauge gravel would find its way, via the bottom of people's shoes, into the house. If you have to have a narrow-gauge gravel, setting it into tarmac can be a fine solution, but for most people, this is prohibitively expensive. So, large-gauge gravel of the correct depth is the solution for me.

Of course, the weeds are delighted with me for providing them with a water-retentive gravel mulch and must be removed, but on the other hand hollyhocks, poppies, linaria and love-in-a-mist like it and, other than along the drive, these are left so that the gravel around the house has become just an excuse for yet more garden.

Photographs

In our second winter, I had to face another winter storm. One that had gathered more or less since the day we moved in, ominous and threatening, but until that second winter distant and somehow capable of being partly disregarded.

It had been during the period when we were preparing to move that we became acutely aware of clouds on the horizon. My mother hadn't been right for a while and via a series of unpleasant interviews with doctors it was established that she had lung cancer. This was evidenced from an X-ray because she pointedly refused to let them do anything else to her. In a rather old-fashioned way she seemed to accept her circumstances and the last thing she wanted was for modern medicine to poke, prod and irradiate her into feeling worse. She soldiered on and ignored any advice that was given to her by conventional medical practitioners.

In the summer, our family GP gently suggested we should reckon on having her around until Christmas. In the event, she smashed the predictions by a full country mile, lasting eighteen months longer than anyone had expected. Good old Mum.

My mother was evacuated from London during the war. She boarded a train to Oxford aged two and would never see her own mother again. Her father came to collect her after the war but her mother (a fiery Irish lady called Bridie, which is almost all we know about her) was never mentioned again. I now understand that my mother carried a well of pain around caused by the loss of her mother for the rest of her life. I don't blame her. The fact her mother had just disappeared (in a conspiracy between adults) as opposed to, for example, more straightforwardly dying, I am sure made the sense of abandonment worse.

Somehow my mother emerged from this train crash of a childhood to become a famous model, in the decade immediately prior to the one in which Twiggy elevated being a famous model to something akin to a film star. At some point I was considered old enough and I was shown the small folio of photographs that dated from my mother's modelling days. For someone who had been photographed incessantly over a decade or more she had kept very few shots for posterity.

I know she had been photographed incessantly because on one occasion, long before I was born, an argument between my parents was resolved when my father, on his way to the airport, passed a billboard with my mother on it holding a loaf of Hovis bread. He felt so guilty after the row they had just had, he cancelled his trip, turned around and went back to make up. My mother giggled as she told me the story. I remember sitting wide-eyed at the end of her bed and hearing about what seemed to me to be the deep past. Stories from a time before technicolour, a time when people and events shuddered through existence in black and white. I also know from looking at her narrow little folio of pictures that my mother was a great beauty. She was achingly beautiful, so beautiful it must have caused her problems, in the same way that a billionaire might find it hard to know a true from a false friend. Albeit with plenty of Irish and Welsh thrown in for good measure, she was, every inch, an English rose.

My parents had a passionate though stormy relationship. When their marriage broke down my mother (who nursed me as an infant in her fifties) told me that she had no interest in another relationship because no one could possibly match up to my father. Again, I didn't realise it as a child, but I now see she was utterly broken-hearted. She gave no sign of having any romantic impulse for the rest of her life. She did, however, spend time with me in our little London garden, and I remember planting an apple tree of which we both became immeasurably proud. Somewhere there is a photograph of it, and another of me eating its first rosy red apple. The link between horticulture and healing was established early on.

I don't have that many photographs of my mother. Having been incessantly photographed in her early years she recoiled from being archived as she grew into her later years. As the storm of her illness mounted, I began finding it hard to look at photographs of her without feeling intense pain.

But I had another photograph of my favourite rose that gave me strength that winter. In fact, I spend a lot of the winter looking at the summer, as if from the wrong side of a pane of glass. This is because every year I take thousands of photographs of the garden and there are always one or two that seem to stand out and become a source of sustenance. These get pulled up on my computer screen and stared at repeatedly. In the short, harsh days, I need this. But I don't allow myself the therapy until after Christmas, in the same way that I never allowed myself to think about home until the day before term finished. The darkest part of the night is always immediately before the dawn.

That winter it was a photograph of my favourite rose. It was one of the few roses that was growing here before we came and I am not entirely sure what it is, nor why I like it so much. Sometimes I feel furtive because I am aware that people might consider this behaviour odd. It is not odd to look at photos, but odd perhaps to look at the same one again and again. I am not conscious of why that single image seems to hold within its patina the whole gamut of summer and hope; of what else I was doing or thinking when I pulled the shutter down; of where else I might have seen those colours or that shape before. But the image of that rose helped me stand against the gathering storm.

These days, I put roses for the house in one of two polished silver tankards I am lucky enough to own. In fact, one tankard is mine and the other I have on temporary loan from my son, who received it as a christening present. The tankards get their annual polish when the first roses break. I particularly like deep-red roses sitting alongside ice-white ones, all set off by the play of light on sparkling silver. The way light plays across silver is enrapturing, and something that I at least can't capture in a photograph. For a long time I didn't put red and white roses together because it was a colour combination my mother hated. I heard at the end of her bed about how it reminded her of the Blitz. I asked her why. She looked at me quizzically and then explained, without spelling it out. Red and white are, of course, the colours of a bombing raid. But these days I grow a dedicated patch of the red rose Darcey Bussell and the white Winchester Cathedral near to the kitchen for picking. Thankfully it was not my Blitz, nor my war; I know it only through photographs, and they are black and white.

Lost worlds

All my life I have been carrying around a special box into which I have placed all the tricky, difficult feelings. I had marked the box with a label that read 'Unpack when you get home'. For me a real home could only be in the country, and I think my sense had been that this box could only be safely unpacked when I arrived in it.

The parts of my early childhood that I spent with my mother in London were not awful but they were thin and watery like midwinter light. In high summer here, the sun crosses main avenue late in the evening, but now it has a mean, narrow arc; it peeps sheepishly over the holly hedge and fuddles off rudely back in the general direction of Oxford without even bothering to stay for tea. It is not that winter sun doesn't bear gifts, but that it seems to be without any real sense of itself. That is how I felt about living in London. I missed my dad. I would visit him in the country at weekends but until I was seven my school was in London and therefore so was I. I always wanted to be in the country.

I remember my father visiting us in London. It was my birthday and my heart leapt as I heard someone say: 'David is at the door.' In he swept followed by a chauffeur carrying the largest, reddest remote-control car I had ever seen. My father stood by the cooker for a period but I could tell the normality of the situation was getting to him. After five minutes he left. His immaculate car sped off down our street. As it accelerated rapidly the pain of not sitting next to him in the back seat increased.

I was well aware of the fact that my desire to be with him and in the countryside as much as possible (he was only ever in London for three days a week) equated to abandoning my mother to her more or less solitary city life. The island of longing to escape to the country, and to the soil, sat within a sea of guilt about abandoning my mum. These are not feelings I would want my children to have to parse, but of course kids up and down the country do.

Visiting London now, even for a work meeting, often brings up those forgotten though not entirely resolved muddy feelings. This is one part of my emotional core, and it is in my garden where the knots are still occasionally unpicked and the loose ends tied up. Gardens can do this – I don't force it, it just happens. Leaving London remains entirely an escape for me. Visiting is one thing, but I have never, ever, missed living in the place.

I was planted in soil that was almost entirely populated with adults. Weekdays in London with my mother and weekends and the holidays with my father and the coterie of people, from the domestic staff to visiting politicians, that made up his court. There is no question this did me good in lots of ways, but my life was almost entirely devoid of people the same age. I was suckled emotionally by adults, many of whom had more than a passing resemblance to Dr Strangelove.

My father had a so-called 'Peace Garden' filled with old English roses planted in geometrically shaped beds. He knew to choose roses that smelt nice and, when I once remarked on this, I could tell he took pleasure in my having noticed. During the cold war he would entertain spies, generals and politicians in this garden in order to have long conversations about how to defend freedom from the threat of Soviet totalitarianism.

I am grateful to this cast of characters because they were surprisingly kind and patient with me; and in any case they were my social life. There was the odd birthday party, stilted affairs with children I hardly knew, but I hardly remember a single 'play date'. Sybilla, on the other hand, had an endless stream of people her own age passing through her house, many of whom became, and still are, firm friends. Now, thanks to Sybilla, our kids have play dates all the time, and this is something we both feel is really important. Children, like plants, will respond to the soil in which they are planted. Like puppies, they do better if they are socialised.

I once read somewhere that the medieval poor in Europe saw the Pope as a man who lived in a glistening city on the other side of an impossibly large mountain range but had their best interests at heart. Whether this is a dubious claim or not, it sums up how I felt about my father during the early part of my childhood. By the time I could hold a fork properly, things changed, and while there were a few bumps along the road, in the end he became my best friend (he would have hated that language for its sentimentality, but he would have nonetheless acknowledged the sentiment), and certainly he was the person with whom I laughed the most and the person upon whom I sharpened what intellectual metal I have.

That is all now a lost world; but this world, my *eard* and my sky, remain. My love of the *eard* and of *engel lond* where that *eard* is to be found; and of East Anglia, where the sky is biggest, all came directly from my father. In bleakest midwinter, this I still have. Our *eard* sits under an immense sky; and for me looking up has always helped to unravel the knots inside. It has always been a therapy; a cure against the knottiness of self. There is something about that point where the fixed earth meets the floating sky that can bring peace to a fevered and anxious mind. It is why we like sunsets. As the sun rises, and then as it sets, it draws a line through this point of meeting; it reminds us that we must look up as well as down. For me, the sky is a medicine of last resort for when the knots are at their tightest. The medicine is there, winter or summer.

When we arrived here there was no garden below the elm hedge to rise and meet the sky; to lend a human voice to the eternal negotiation between the certain and the uncertain; between the finite and the infinite. There were just acres of virgin soil that jutted out into, and provided almost 360-degree views of, the Peb Valley. Because of the peculiar topography, the whole five-acre meadow seemed to hover like a floating island within an impossibly large sky: a garden moated by cloud. We quickly started to call this space 'the skymeadow', which soon became just 'skymeadow'. My struggle to create a new garden, to bring harmony back, to say to my father with plants what I could no longer say to him with words has been fought on this *eard* and under this sky.

Spring

The ground begins to quiver

At a certain point in the spring, the sun gains enough height to throw light via an external window through some modern coloured glass that sits in the door that leads to my study. The result is a rainbow of colour spread across the herringbone brickwork of our kitchen floor. Just in the afternoon. Just for a short while. This happens about the time the birdsong increases in intensity and it reminds me that soon daffodils will be massed down by the holly hedge and swathes of them will seem to glow, caught in the evening light.

The fact that our home is slap-bang in the middle of undulating English countryside, and is full of children, dogs and cats (and, of course, that I share it with my wife), makes it the only place I truly want to be. That is true in each season, but there is no denying that we both get a real boost when spring ambles along. It never comes quickly enough. At some point we know the sun will be high enough to crest the chestnut tree, and large enough to spread a little warmth, and then the conditions will be right for us to have morning tea together at the little table in the courtyard. This moment brings a feeling of palpable relief. Doors start to get left open and the children can roam free once again. The decibel level within the house dramatically reduces. For me, spring is a busy time and my office is cluttered with pots and seed trays and little seedlings, starting out on the journey that will lead, via the coldframes, into the garden.

Of course, horticulturally speaking, spring starts almost imperceptibly, but each day I look keenly for its signs. Snowdrops, widely marketed as the heralds of spring (especially by those with large gardens open to the public), are to my mind an unreliable guide. It is true that snowdrops won't break through soil that is frozen solid (nothing will) but they will break well before spring wins its tussle with winter. I don't allow myself to celebrate the change of the season until the primroses slather themselves like a thick buttery spread along the sides of the ancient country lanes that surround Skymeadow; to do otherwise would be to court disappointment. Primroses are the true heralds of spring.

As their name suggests, primroses are the 'prime' or 'first' rose of the season. Many of the lanes around Skymeadow have been functioning highways and byways from as far back as the Iron Age, and I enjoy the thought that the primroses have been delighting wayfarers since then. Each individual flower has a line of descent that was already well established before men and women arrived in these isles. Originally the lanes around here would have been hewn (or trampled) from surrounding woodland, and it is precisely this edge of woodland habitat that primroses seem to relish. Most plants that flower in early spring have evolved to do their photosynthesis

90

on the woodland floor before trees break leaf and block out the light. This is their niche and it is why they perform early in the season. It is also why they tend to like the loose, leafy soil that is common on a woodland floor.

When the temperature is reliably above 8°C, things grow. The three major influences on plant growth are: light, temperature and water. This is why in the tropics everything grows at three times the rate. When I started gardening I wanted to grow the widest possible range of plants in the greatest numbers possible. The result was often a large number of poorly grown plants, or simply lots of dead plants.

At some point, I made a subtle (or not so subtle) shift. I found I had an increasing desire to grow less but better; to stretch my skills as a gardener. This meant really concentrating on a smaller number of plants to ensure I got the very best specimens at the end. Whether you are defoliating a tomato to let sunlight at the fruit, choosing when to sow a vegetable or adding increasing quantities of horticultural grit to your potting compost, it always turns on thinking carefully about light, temperature and water. A basic tip is that sowing plants whose growth hinges on light early is pointless – they will grow weak until the days lengthen – so you might as well leave them until then. I find basil is one such plant. On the other hand, plants that need a long growing season to mature, such as tomatoes or cucumbers, are worth starting slightly earlier than seems comfortable.

During our first spring, the simple and primordial delight I take each year from this moment of quiver – this moment when my potting mixtures, pots and seeds come out – was overshadowed by the now apparently rapid decline in my mother's prognosis. It was becoming increasingly clear that the time we would have left with her was sadly limited. It was reaching the point where moving her became sufficiently hard

91

(and painful for her) that the net benefit of a visit here was dropping below the water line. We hoped Sybilla would get her driving licence before we hit this point, which would mean I would have fewer school runs to do and could have more freedom to travel up to London to see Mum. I felt the approach of a cloud. A mounting sense of split loyalty. The odd tension between home and mother. London and country. Those old muddy feelings from childhood; but shortly with dire and permanent consequence.

My brothers were both living in London at the time and were making a sterling effort to enrich every last second of the life that Mum had left to live. I wasn't living in London, I had just moved heaven and earth to try and get out of London, which I could see might very shortly leave my conscience with those old jagged edges.

Still, the quiver was on, the ground was teetering on the edge of becoming its true self again. Little nodules of green were frisking up like horses at the start of a race, waiting for the sound of the starter's gun. Soon the race would be on and we would move to a time when the garden can change, almost, over the course of a day. Before that, however, the fruit trees would try their very hardest to mesmerise the early pollinators. This was a distraction I longed for and knew that I needed. I resolved that this spring, if Mum couldn't come to the garden, I would take the garden to her.

The rose garden

The little flowerbeds by the magnolia tree, dug in the first winter, had been a start. But if they had been the smallest taster, during our first spring I started consuming the garden and its potential in earnest. I knew that what this new garden would need was a beating heart, a figurative centre of operations and a floral focus. So, during that first spring I went for the jugular and dug the new rose garden. Against the various emotional pressures I was living with at the time, it was a great therapy.

Gardening has taught me that you can dig for victory, but you can also dig for mental health. The days I spent wrestling with the soil in the rose garden, cutting turf, double digging and digging in compost and manure were the days in which I mourned the loss of my parents. Every year the rose garden starts again from a new and more secure base as roses use the root growth they achieved in the previous season to reach yet more magnificence. Now, three years on, they respond thick and fast to growing temperature in the spring.

I used to stand in the rose garden, out of breath, covered in sweat, and suddenly well up. I trampled my tears into the same soil that now provides us with billowing foliage and tall flower spikes in the summer. The rose garden is a story of hope: it has enabled me to turn loss into gain. Despite their differences, both my parents would have immediately and intuitively understood the attempt to extract meaning in this way. The steely and sinewy effort not just to grow plants, sometimes in adverse conditions, but also to grow meaning and purpose at the same time on the side of a hill. I felt their pleasure as I dug the rose garden. I believe they would be proud of Skymeadow generally.

My name for the rose garden is 'The Isles'. This is pretentious, I see that, but I don't care. Our gardens are protected places in which we can be as flamboyant or demure as we wish and pretence is so often how the creative urge manifests initially. A metaphorical 'river' runs through Skymeadow (down from the house, and along main avenue) and The Isles is where it breaks and eddies. This imagined river is the backbone off which the structure of Skymeadow has coalesced. The rose garden is called The Isles because of my personal romantic attachment to the Western Isles, and specifically the memories I have of being in Scotland with my father. It is The Isles because it is the beating heart of Skymeadow; and Skymeadow is itself an island, and water washes us as it washes against us.

I wanted the rose garden to celebrate, to overflow with abundance and to sing a song of hope. I wanted it to do that thing our hearts do when they are overflowing with gratitude and wonder. I decided to dedicate swathes of it to my favourite, quintessentially English and very simple spring succession: richly coloured tulips dancing away above clouds of violet forget-me-nots interspersed with roses holding in their healthy foliage all the promise of summer to come. If you add the first true warmth of a spring sun, the chorus of birds looking for love and the smell of freshly cut grass, perhaps even heaven starts to break in.

This simple progression of flowers holds for me more than I am truly capable of expressing. It was a bed like this in Gloucestershire that first slayed me with wonder and made me want to garden all the time. For some peculiar reason this floral succession is where, for me, a love of gardening, as opposed to a deeper and earlier love for the countryside, set in.

My entire flower gardening to date has been somehow anchored by the desire to create this one simple but mysterious formula, and then to enjoy it as it improves each year. The sense of its return, each year better than the last, is more than half the pleasure I take from it. I tried it in a miniature scale in London, and I am well into creating it here on a somewhat more sumptuous scale in the rose garden. Everything else in the garden is mysteriously subservient to this single moment of wonder and waking up in the gardening year: tulips, forget-me-nots and all the promise of roses to come.

In the spring, the beds in the rose garden, like similar ones around the country, remind me that in answer to Rupert Brooke: yes, there will be honey still for tea! For me, spring captures a wider hope that courses through all our veins. Those flowers remind me that together we can improve the lot of those in our communities who have nothing; the widow and the orphan. They remind me that while sadness and anxiety exist, no one need experience them alone. In short, this little rose garden, which I have pretentiously named The Isles and in effect amounts to four large beds and a splay of topiary, seems to hold the world in its tiny hands. Odd, but there it is.

Casting a vision

During our first spring, when the garden began to lurch excitedly into growth and I would wander off for hours and hours of digging, mostly in the new rose garden, and afterwards adding flowerbeds around the house, plans and ideas for every square inch of the garden were being bandied around constantly. Over meals and after dinner, I would gabble away happily attempting to share the better parts of my visual imagination with Sybilla (and, frankly, anyone else who was polite enough to listen or happened to be visiting). For me, this was a period of immense excitement, such that when I woke up in the morning I would have to go immediately out, out into the garden.

In the same way as an artist will sketch and then adjust before sketching some more, or a painter will build up his canvas in layers making minute adjustments as he goes, this is what a gardener does too. I will cast a vision, hone it, play with it, turn it round in my mind, reject parts of it, add in others. I am fortunate that I can lay plants out on a flowerbed in my mind and watch them grow and develop. I can see six months or two years hence and wind backwards and forwards as if I was playing a video. I sometimes feel in this way like Gandalf, striding through Middle-earth switching, swapping and adjusting with my staff as I go. In fact, I enjoy planting trees in my mind as I walk around the place; using my staff to cast out great avenues and then tearing them up again (that bit is fun too), rolling out great new swathes of pristine turf to cover over the scarred, abandoned planting holes and re-planting the avenue elsewhere. All this I can do, and I enjoy doing. I need silence. If someone starts speaking to me, the world evaporates and I am back.

Some people like rugby, others like needlework; I like playing with my visual imagination. As I look back, I think my father's imagination worked like this too. It was never discussed – why would it be? But he was always making 'improvements' and would drive slowly around the farm silently looking, for hours and hours. I would often sit next to him in the car. I know now what he was doing. He identified most with a keen-eyed eagle. He loved flying, he loved the sky: he was a pilot. He was proud that as a family we all had pilot's vision. Now I see this highly visual component in myself and increasingly in my son. My brothers have it too. I suspect almost all people can use their visual imagination in this way, at least to a certain extent. But some, I have discovered, find it harder than others.

During that first spring, as I excitedly tried to share my plans with Sybilla (probably at a rate, volume and intensity that was quite unfair), I noticed she would quite frequently look blankly back at me. I might have taken it as a lack of interest on her part, even an uncharacteristic lack of generosity about something that clearly excited me, but for the fact that I recognised within her not a refusal to be excited, but a void from which excitement was struggling to emerge. She kept asking me to draw things for her rather than explain them, in itself not an unreasonable request. Then I realised I had seen this before.

An old friend of my father was utterly and completely incapable of visualising something unless it was drawn for him. He was probably also the most brilliant and intelligent person I have ever met. He had worked in and around the military during the cold war and, with no exaggeration, had played a central role in a number of critical moments in world history. But he could never see something unless I sketched it for him. I suddenly realised Sybilla and he had this same thing, whatever it was. On the other hand, Sybilla could probably learn a completely new language in a month, whereas despite years of lessons I can barely string a sentence together in French.

At university some educational consultant had arranged a standard test for Sybilla as part of her course. After the test, she had been told she was severely dyspraxic. We had always thought it a bit of a joke, not really knowing (or either of us caring) what it might mean. It didn't seem to make any practical difference to our lives. Sybilla got a great degree, she can speak several languages (something that my father's friend was also able to do), she is a successful freelance journalist and now the mother of four kids. She is very, very intelligent and also wise. So what if she was dyspraxic? Still, I remember that first spring suddenly realising that Sybilla had some sort of block in her ability to visualise, to organise spatially, particularly when being asked to do so from words. I just remember noticing this, and thinking of my

99

father's friend, and wondering if this was all somehow linked to this thing called dyspraxia and wondering if it might somehow affect our plans in a wider way that I hadn't anticipated yet.

Beyond roses

I wanted the rose garden to be more than just that. I wanted it to be a place to discover exotic-looking flowers in among the roses. It is surprising just how exotic-looking certain ordinary English garden flowers are when you stop and stare at them. I find the geometry of the harlequin bonnet of a snake's-head fritillary unspeakably pleasing, but that such a thing should be native to Britain? Or the way lupins build swirling citadels of colour high into the sky – they mass to look like a colourful medieval Italian city. Opium poppies, so blush, so blowsy, sitting atop their equally beguiling glaucous foliage and carrying in their sap the power to take away pain (though it is a criminal offence to harvest the resin). If you stop and look hard at a simple sweet pea you will see an orchid-like creature that reeks with a sort of exotic fecundity; a determination to survive so strong that it has the power to mesmerise even *Homo sapiens*.

That we can have all this hope on our doorstep causes my heart to skip a beat. Sweet peas are sown when it is still winter outside, but this is where the journey back towards summer starts. They hold a special place in my heart and garden. I used to go on holiday with my wife's family to Cornwall every summer and in our room was a botanical drawing of a sweet pea. I can see it clearly now. This was about the time that I started to garden with real intent, and it was before I had experienced personal loss. Many couples have a happy place and ours is Cornwall. Sweet peas are where I went to start the long internal march back to summer. It is amazing how much therapy can be found within the pages of a sweet-pea catalogue.

In London, I managed to pack several hundred sweet peas into our little back garden, and the first clutch of them placed on each of the children's bedside tables marked the true start of summer. When sweet peas start to flower I go around every five days taking each flower off in the hope none will set seed and bring the display to a premature halt. This isn't a chore; it is a ritual.

One year in London I grew three rows of them to make living walls for a pop-up gazebo in which we had a little party to celebrate our third daughter's christening. The air was heavy with their scent.

Now I stuff every conceivable receptacle in the house with them and any left over get a dollop of soggy tissue paper around the base of their stems and are then wrapped in tin foil to be given to friends. I like to gather a really generous posy of sweet peas, with a girth as wide as I can manage, and shove it into the hands of a neighbour.

There are as many varieties, almost, as stars in the sky, but the sweet pea I grow every year without fail is Matucana. It is the original sweet pea introduced to England in the seventeenth century by a monk called Francis Cupani and it is still the sweet pea with the strongest scent.

This spring the rose garden has other lush or exotic-looking flowers coming: lupins, kniphofia, delphiniums, geraniums, clematis, sea holly, dahlias, dark blue gladioli, poppies, nasturtiums, cornflowers and love-in-a-mist.

I have always felt attracted not just to exotic flowers, but also to exotic foliage, and I wanted this for the rose garden too. I have a red banana plant that goes out for the summer and comes into my study during the winter. If I had large runs of glasshouses or a giant orangery, like the great estates did, I would have an army of bananas to set out each summer, but for now I have just one. Even so, it causes me a disproportionate amount of pleasure. If I had a smaller city garden, I might try leaving more exotic plants like the hardier bananas outside for the winter, with the benefit of a jumper made from horticultural fleece. One of the great joys of gardening in London was the microclimate; my tulips came out a month or two earlier than they do now. I wish I had thought to experiment with the more tender plants while I had the chance. If I was gardening in London now (or any other big city with a microclimate), I would try to push these boundaries.

Despite the restrictions of our climate, there is plenty of hardy exotic foliage to be had too. A large number of figs are hardy, as are castor oil plants, which have exotic fig-like foliage. Castor oil plants also happen to be one of the common garden plants that are genuinely poisonous, so if you have children or animals proceed with caution. There are less usual fig trees available too, such as Ice Crystal, whose foliage is jagged and divided as per its name.

I love cannas, particularly the ones with red leaves that, when in full swing, look like the leaves on a banana. They have the added advantage of exotic flowers provided late in the season. I get away with leaving them in the ground over winter under a thick blanket of compost, but this wouldn't be possible in all locations in the UK. What they do need is plenty of sunlight in the summer. I really wanted the rose garden to include all this exotic abundance so that it might be a spectacle at the heart of the garden; the place in the garden of perpetual celebration. But, even now, three years in, when I start to think like this, it just reminds me how much there is still to do.

It wasn't to be until the rose garden entered its third growing season that it began to take on a fullness that hinted towards what I had originally imagined. By then, the roses looked full, the carpet of forget-me-nots at their ankles unfurled without bare patches, the box topiary sported regular draughts of light green growth, things began to meet in midair as they grew, and a new fullness descended. Albeit immaturely, once the sense of the garden unmistakably arrived, something shifted within me. The initial thrill of simply bringing something into being, of lighting the tinder if you like, was replaced by a fuller, deeper and electrically exciting sense of meeting; like hearing the first cry of a newborn.

Back in our first spring, when all the beds in the rose garden were freshly dug and planted, and everything looked terribly small, we had a setback just as the rose buds were looking fat and full of promise. One morning as I made my daily pass I noticed that every single bud had been neatly clipped off. Every single one. My heart sank. I had forgotten to shut the bottom gate and the blasted deer had snuck in with a ruthless and targeted efficiency. This, however, is a useful reminder that, unlike painting or writing, gardening takes place across four dimensions. To the ordinary three you must add time. The canvas moves, the words on the page only agree to remain sitting for a certain period of time. Everything, even the end product (especially the end product), is in flux.

104

Flower shows (such as the Chelsea Flower Show, the Olympics of horticulture) are a conceit in the sense that they attempt to pretend away the vagaries of this fourth dimension. But it is not possible, other than for a week at a time. Nothing in a garden sits still. Some people have tried to recreate Chelsea show gardens at home, but regrettably they are doomed to failure. Even Louis XIV at Versailles couldn't do it, though perhaps he got closest. My whole attempt at building a garden in Skymeadow runs in the opposite direction; time with its tragedies and triumphs, but always with its pleasing perpetual motion, is at the centre. No attempt is made to dam it. Playing any other game seems to me not just brittle and phoney, but pointless.

Most of the work in the rose garden now happens in the spring, when there is a rush of weeding and mulching. I have come to the conclusion that it is preferable to mulch later rather than earlier, at the end of March, or even into April, because the weed-suppressing effect lasts longer into the season and the nutrients the plant receives come at a more useful time. A later mulch also enables the soil to soak up as much of the spring rain as possible before the top covering goes on – important for us because we garden in the driest part of the UK. March is a month with wild weather; as country folk used to say, 'In like a lion, out like a lamb'. Over the course of half an hour spent weeding the rose garden in March, I have seen hail, rainstorm, blue skies and blistering sun. I planted the yew topiary on just such a day and I remember at one point our dog Seymour and I had to run for shelter because the hail had become so menacing; shortly afterwards my shirt was off as I dug the next planting hole. March is a month of battle – a new season battles the old, and the old doesn't retreat without a fight.

A *place apart*

While Sybilla and I both sit at different and perhaps extreme ends of the spectrum with respect to the way we visualise and manage space, in practical terms it has a very similar effect. Space, which tumbles into a deeper sense of place, matters deeply to both of us. I found it very hard to find anything of myself in among the busyness of a city. I found it hard to feel myself within the busyness of grief. I needed a place apart. Sybilla did too. This is what the rose garden is all about. We needed an island that we could retreat to and in some way share with those we had loved, admired and lost. Place is somehow a vector for this sharing, and at the same time an invitation to start the slow process of rebuilding; of repairing the damage that had been wrought to our internal citadels by swingeing loss. This is why I set about building the rose garden and why it felt so urgent when we first arrived.

Scent will deliver a sense of place instantly; and a place apart too. I did plenty of farming with my father, but not much gardening. I watched from a safe distance as he waged a merciless war against the greenfly in the greenhouse, and I watched, also from a safe distance, as he engaged in the only other bit of gardening that he felt was worthy of his direct attention: pruning. This was carried out with great thought and far too much fury. My father was every bit a countryman but I think he felt gardening was drab. Probably something like farming for children. He would have found an herbaceous border fiddly, but he was keyed into the power of horticulture to deliver scent. He allowed great beds of lavender by the house so that in the summer the smell would waft in through open windows. And he loved scented roses, and he loved scented daffodils, all this we had in common, and all these things now confer to me a sense of place; moreover, place as it should be.

I am not one who objects to daffodil flowers (some people do) but it is their scent that slays me with wonder each year when I first catch it in the garden. Last year, I turned a corner and the mingled scent of daffodils, Christmas box and hamamelis stopped me in my tracks. I dropped to the ground and just sat. The smell of daffodils takes me back to my childhood. My father would have vast vases of daffodils placed on practically every spare table surface and all the way down the centre of the long dining-room table. This was spring indoors, as the lambs gambolling in the fields was spring outdoors. This was place.

My father's favourite daffodil was the typical exemplar: I think Dutch Master, also sometimes marketed as King Alfred. It has a big, brash yellow flower with a big brash yellow trumpet and visually does absolutely everything a daffodil should do. In this garden, I grow literally dozens (perhaps fifty) different varieties of daffodil and I recently picked from the widest possible range and bundled them all into a china cachepot with a girth of about twenty inches. It was wondrous and it reminded me that I find the diversity and abundance of a happy acre, available for picking even in early spring, deeply comforting. This too is place.

Sometimes you need to go away in order to come back; you need to take yourself into a different world in order to find yourself in the current one. My garden is very much about this process. The notion of a garden as set apart from the humdrum of ordinary life is important to both Sybilla and myself, and important for this process. Coleridge's 'suspension of disbelief' that you hope to find in the theatre must also take place in the heart of a visitor for a garden to be enjoyed to the maximum. If this suspension of disbelief is entered into willingly, the best gardens, and even a simple stretch of hedgerow, can have the power to tilt reality slightly on its edge.

For example, I have always loved the common dog rose. This is the rose that flowers along Britain's hedgerows in May. In fact, it is my favourite of all roses. In the rose garden, along the hedge closest to the house, its delicate little flowers spangle against the still fresh leaves of the field maple, elm and oak. When massed, the effect is both soft and overwhelming; like a million little fairy pools along the side of the hedge. You can imagine the little fairies leaping from pool to pool in the evening sun. They produce exquisitely elegant hips of the brightest red, easily a match for any holly. Their leaves smell of apples.

I have shards of memory that seem, despite being outwardly innocuous, to hold more meaning than I can describe; like icebergs, their true content is somewhere below water level. I remember my father, on a bright May evening, explaining that 'dog' merely meant 'common' as we drove slowly up a hedgerow in the Land Rover. Who knows what else I had done that day? Perhaps I had just returned from an epic and happy march with my lurcher Tigger? Or perhaps my father had conferred a sense of approval on me simply because I had been taking an interest in what grew in the hedge? Something gave me a special affection for this most ordinary, though beautiful, rose. Something endowed it with the ability to deliver to me a profound sense of place. For me, the dog rose is rooted somewhere below the water line, somewhere in the iceberg.

Species roses, of which the dog rose is one, are so called because they are the group of wild roses from which all the cultivated varieties have been bred. They contain roses with some quite unusual characteristics such as *Rosa sericea subsp. omeiensis f. pteracantha*, better (and certainly more easily) referred to as the winged thorn rose whose thorns are giant crimson, bat-like things. Or *Rosa x cantabrigiensis* whose yellow flowers are early and whose delicate, ferny foliage I adore. Species roses have another huge benefit for an organic gardener like me: they tend to be disease resistant. If you want an impermeable barrier with real visual interest, grow species roses in hawthorn. Over the last three years I have been building just this combination within the hedges that surround the rose garden; as a result, it is assuming a greater sense of place.

The rose garden is protected by hawthorn on two sides, the southerly and westerly. This is ideal because it fools the prevailing southwesterly wind, which for most of the year is generous with its presence. I have used the hedges around the rose garden, both those that were here when we arrived and the new ones I have planted, to create and foster a sense of splendid isolation. This makes Coleridge's willing suspension of disbelief easier to enter into. It makes the sense of a place apart an easier prize. Gardens are, at their most basic, enclosures; a quality brought into quivering and obvious relief by those that are moated, such as the famous one at Helmingham Hall. All this otherness builds a sense of place.

Lately, I have had a growing sense of the vast East Anglian sky lapping up against the edges of Skymeadow, and the edges of the rose garden itself. On misty days the garden feels like an island outcrop held above a perilous and impenetrable sea. I have a growing sense that Skymeadow has a moat, but it is one provided by the sky. My father laid a road through the farm that we lived on that ran up a hill. When you drove on it, for a moment, you had the sense it led into the sky. He loved this conceit. So did I. I used to tease him about how clever he had been for having the idea, by heaping on him exaggerated and hyperbolic praise.

I have also come to realise that Skymeadow is in some mysterious way a shared endeavour between my father and me. This is because it is a place in a sense that we would both have recognised. We may be separated by time and the fact of his absence, but in some profound way this doesn't stop me sharing a sense of place with him. The rose garden has taught me that time and absence don't amount to much when set against the irreducible bond between a father and his son. All this speaks to grief, but it also speaks to self and to the proper order of things. Place apart becomes a vector for both courage and comfort; for renewing, rebuilding, covenanting again. Place apart is where my grief and my hope meet, it is where human business can be done; it is where I am a gardener, a grieving son, and a loving father. It is where Sybilla and I can sit together. In some way place is the loving heart of a person. It is spring all year long in the rose garden; here hope and sap rise eternal.

Stuck

During our first spring at Peverels reality came rushing at us. We had to face a mounting practical dilemma. My business was parlous before the move, but I knew that with a huge investment of time and effort I could set it straight. However, I couldn't make a huge investment in either time or effort unless Sybilla got a nanny or a driving licence soon. The mechanics of managing a large young family in a rural location were increasingly plain.

Sybilla had always resisted having a nanny at all costs. In fact, it is almost the only material thing we have ever really disagreed on. I have always argued we should have more childcare, while Sybilla has always had a visceral urge to do all the childcare herself. Many people who have four small children under a certain age also have a parent or grandparent (or even a kindly older lady) somewhere vaguely proximate. At the time, we didn't.

I have always argued that, in the past, most people would have been born and bred in a village, and some would never have travelled any further than the nearest town. They would have been raised among uncles, aunts, cousins and local eccentrics. Unlike today, they would not have been parented exclusively by their parents. This dream of community is not simply a romantic wish; it is how life was for millennia. In modern times, we approximate this via help, either paid or from within the family.

When we were in London we did have the odd au pair but with a few exceptions, through no fault of their own, they had always made Sybilla depressed. We now realise that for dyspraxics space, particularly the intimate space within a home, is unusually important; and this extends to who they have to share it with. Nonetheless, I argued on. Given that my parents had gone, and hers, although they helped as best they could, lived busy lives miles away in Gloucestershire, couldn't we just get the odd bit of afternoon help? Or the odd night where we had help at bathtime? My lack of earnings didn't help build my case. In the meantime, Sybilla kept saying that she hoped to get her driving licence within a month or two, after which the nanny would be surplus to requirements, so what would be the point of hiring one only to then dismiss them?

I gladly acquiesced because, though I kept going through the motions with regards to growing my business, deep down I didn't really want it to work and my ties at home were a useful foil. In fact, perhaps subconsciously, I now think I wanted my business to shrink to the very thin point that it eventually arrived at. Helping out at home was the perfect excuse for gradual failure. I wanted to garden, I wanted to grieve, and I needed to do both in isolation; almost regardless of the cost.

Still, in that first year, I remember dropping the girls at nursery, then dropping Isaac at his school and going down to London on the train for meetings knowing I would have to be back at 3 p.m. to pick them all up. After this was tea, if I was lucky some digging, responding to emails then bathtime and bedtime, then more emails late into the night. Trying to pursue a business career in these circumstances was hard, but it was also ultimately pointless. I knew, Sybilla knew, we both knew, that my heart was no longer in it; we just hadn't managed to admit it to each other. Untangling exactly what that meant and would ultimately look like was still a year off. In the meantime, we were lucky to have savings from our time in London.

During that 'stuck' period, even though we were neither of us able to have the conversation in an entirely honest way, we would often discuss my work and what my next steps should be. I knew increasingly clearly that I wanted to garden, and write about gardens, full time. This caused subtle, and not so subtle, friction. Not so much because the desire was in itself wrong, but because it was different from what we had planned, particularly my previous protestations that I would happily conduct a daily commute down to London and carry on in a sensible occupation. Our discussions ranged back and forth over the options.

Neither of us are particularly materialistic, not in the sense that we should be congratulated for our purity, but in the sense that we both genuinely derive most of our pleasure from the simple things: cups of tea, time spent together and our books. I suspect if pushed Sybilla would admit to craving the odd swanky holiday, but neither of us give a fig about cars and accoutrements of that sort. But, of course, it is not just about us: it is about our kids and their futures too. Sybilla has long been a freelance journalist, and she of all people knew that writing was no easy road to riches.

115

The worst aspect of Sybilla not having a driving licence was not my consequent busyness, but her feeling frustrated she couldn't help me. Her driving wasn't progressing quite as planned. Sybilla had started her driving lessons, but she had kicked off with the wrong instructor and there had been a personality clash. She lost her patience and in frustration just booked herself in to do a test in Bury St Edmunds. I knew it was too soon, but I drove her there and paced around the abbey grounds waiting for the outcome. The outcome was not positive. Still, it had only been her first go and she hadn't had the right driving instructor. We picked ourselves up and pushed on.

As one failed driving test moved into another, a dread, imperceptible at first, crept into both our hearts. How many attempts would it take? How long could we afford to wait? With me doing six school runs a day, taking three children there and back in three different directions, we found ourselves googling whether you needed a licence to take a quad bike and trailer on the road. Then it was a lawn mower. We knew things were getting out of hand when we hit 'search' on the legality of operating a mobility scooter, possibly with a trailer attached.

Was everything we had worked for about to come to a shuddering halt? With things as they stood, no nanny and no driving licence, we were stuck. How long could we afford to be stuck, not just financially, but emotionally? How long could Sybilla bear being stuck? The fact that Sybilla, who is frankly independently minded, had to ask me for permission merely to pop to a friend's house or pick up a bottle of milk was brutal. She bore it with impressively calm fortitude. But the thought that we might both be doomed, if not to living in a city, then forever near a bus stop, loomed increasingly large. We began to research how long it had taken other people with dyspraxia to learn to drive. There were stories of ten, twenty or even thirty attempts. We kicked ourselves for not doing all this before, when we were in London, when it couldn't have mattered less.

Of course, Sybilla was also pregnant and, during the second half of her pregnancy, the degree to which we were both stuck increased further. We were told that Sybilla had a low-lying placenta. In itself this is nothing to be particularly concerned about, but in practical terms it meant the doctor advised us that Sybilla should do no lifting. As anyone who has had small children knows, doing almost anything with them without lifting is hard. Moreover, you can't pack a three-year-old off to school in a taxi, at least not every day, so I was picking up the slack. Still, we both kept on in the hope the driving licence would come next month. Despite the low-lying placenta, Sybilla took her sixth test a day before going into labour. It was a fail. Both of us cried.

In among all of this was the growing fact of my mother's grave illness. Another unintended consequence of my being stuck in Essex was that I couldn't be with her in London. Of course, I did make journeys down to see her, and I took her great bundles of lavender to smell, quivers of different roses to see and punnets of gooseberries, raspberries and strawberries to eat. Although she was very ill, smell and taste still gave her great pleasure. But visiting Mum was the same as trying to get away for work; it was all challenging and required mad dashes between school runs. I found the visits painful and difficult. I constantly questioned whether I should have been doing more for her. As with my work, where was the line between the demands of our home life and a sneaking, hidden tendency towards avoidance? It wasn't clear, and into that sliver of a gap crept the old foe, guilt.

Despite the helter-skelter of our lives, that first spring held within its palm a real sense of excitement for me in the garden.

The first spring in a new garden is like arriving at a holiday house at night and then drawing the curtains the next morning to see the view for the first time. I kept making little surprising discoveries as things started to grow. My grief over my father's demise, still very raw, and the anxiety I felt knowing my mother's was shortly before us, meant that I was frequently digging through tears. I found the physical act of digging deeply restorative, along with the sweat and dirt.

By degrees, I began to dare to think of gardening as a legitimate way to work. I kept getting close to this when chatting with Sybilla, but only ever in gentle terms and often with less than encouraging results. The fact that her driving licence seemed further away than she might have originally thought made her feel vulnerable, and as things started to go less well with my business, she wondered whether we might have made a terrible mistake. I tried to reassure her.

Often during that period, after long and quite difficult discussions, I would go to bed resolved to do something sensible, like selling insurance. On every single occasion when I went to bed inwardly pledging to do just such a thing I would dream long and vividly of the garden here. In one dream, I stepped out of the house into a garden that had become a large green cathedral and I was swinging around it on tree branches, defying gravity with each whoop and lunge, experiencing a sensation that seemed as close to real freedom as I was capable of imagining. I knew then, come what may, I could never give gardening up. Any thought of surrender left me feeling thoroughly depressed; but something needed to come along, something that would help me take the leap.

Blossom

As life starts over, as it begins to course through the ground once again (but before growth has started in earnest), the fruit trees blossom in a bid to attract the attention of early pollinators. Their moment is upon us. They need to set their fruit in good time for the long growing season they require. The moment of fertilisation, triggered by the grain of pollen carried on the back of an insect, is the start, whereas the apple (or pear, plum, etc.), in many cases only ripe for harvest in October, is the conclusion.

Here, it is the peach tree that breaks first of all, and always in precarious circumstances, its blossom threatened by a late frost. Last year, the peach tree outside Sybilla's study suddenly died. I grubbed it out with a shovel and inspected the trunk. After cutting it into slices and looking at the wood I concluded it had fallen victim to a combination of peach leaf curl and some unwelcome attention from moths. Of course this was an opportunity to replace it with a new and better variety; and also to give Sybilla a present at the same time.

I chose the variety Peregrine because it is the most likely to perform in our climate and I don't see the point of taking risks with something edgy like a peach. Because peach blossom opens very early, you really want to give it the best possible spot in the garden, which in our case is where the old one was. When the peach blossom opens there are few insects about, so to increase my yield every spring I move from blossom to blossom with a cotton bud dabbing the stamens in imitation of a bee. I have found this dramatically increases the number of peaches.

In the hedges, the first blossom is from the blackthorn, the tree used to fashion a crown of thorns for Jesus and a timely reminder that Easter is within sight. The hawthorn (or 'May' as it was called by country folk) doesn't flower properly until a month later. The popular country saying, 'Don't cast your clout [coat] until May is out', is commonly held to be a reference to the month, but it is in fact a reference to the plant. This year the first blossom came out at the end of April, but I cast my clout well before then.

In the orchard, the plums blossom first, then the pears and finally the apple trees. A giant pear tree, sixty feet in height, lies in the centre of the lawn directly below the house and its white blossom makes a stark and thrilling contrast to the hedges around the lawn, still leafless and transparent. This year I worked in the garden all day, only noticing the tree was in flower in the afternoon on my way back up to the house from Skymeadow. That's how it is, blossom. One minute it isn't there and the next it is. The suddenness of its reveal magnifies the shocking quality of its beauty. Blossom is a sort of visual helium; it makes me feel light, and feeling light and surprised is so much better than just feeling light.

The cherries that run along the boundary of Skymeadow break an ice-white blossom shortly after the pear tree on the lawn of the home garden. By this stage, the white blossom of the blackthorn runs all the way along the northern edge of Skymeadow too. From the pears in the orchard above the barn to the bottom of the meadow, all is white. The month of Lent is one of crystal-white purity in the garden here, at least among the flowering trees that encircle us.

The blossom of the pear tree falls as suddenly as it opens and completely covers the grass in the home garden for a moment. The children pretend it is a covering of snow, which makes a good game for a day or two. Sybilla says it looks like confetti after a regal wedding. She longs for the garish pink blossom, provided by a tree such as Kanzan, a favourite of front gardens up and down the country. I do too, though more secretly. I plan to plant one next autumn.

Twenty yards above my study is a chestnut tree that is very large. I was astonished when I discovered that the chestnut, that bastion of an English upbringing, is in fact entirely foreign; it was imported from France in the seventeenth century. It wasn't brought here because the Stuarts and early Georgians liked a game of conkers, but because it is one of the great flowering trees. Vast spikes flecked with pink; a thousand fecund little warriors marching skyward; a spring display of sheer exoticism. I had to live next to one before I truly saw beyond my schoolboy obsession with conkers.

This is also the time of year for the posy. I love a posy on my desk and it need have no more than a single snowdrop, primrose, violet, snake's-head fritillary, dog's tooth violet, a scrap of blossom or early forget-me-not in it. I have little vases and eggcup-like containers that I use specifically for spring posies. They come just in time to lift one's spirits after a long hard winter, and their delicate promise can be just as lovely as a full bunch of flowers in high summer. Luckily, I have enough of these flowers growing throughout the garden to feed my desire for spring posies, but if I didn't I would have a patch dedicated to growing just these sorts of early wonders.

It is funny how memory associations work; in our second spring, my brother-in-law was staying about the time the peach tree blossomed. After dinner, when we were on our own, both holding a whisky and water, I told him that I had decided to find a way to work in gardening and garden writing full time. Saying the words out loud felt thrilling and also frightening. The feeling had been building up inside me to the point of certain knowledge. I was aware that by speaking beyond Sybilla I was crossing some sort of Rubicon; even if it was within the family. Buoyed up by the wonder of creation and garlanded by the blossom on our little peach tree, and the sure knowledge that within weeks frothing, unavoidable blossom would be all around, I had stepped out and made my decision. He was enthusiastic. He was encouraging. I had no idea, at all, how I might seek to extract from the universe just such a solution.

For a second time, I knew I must proceed, even if it was with Piglet's innocent foolishness. Spring is the time of new beginnings and blossom an invitation to conceive.

Leaf break

While blossom dazzles, it doesn't fill. It is merely an *amuse bouche*, against which leaf break is the main meal. As the leaves unfurl, the country fills; it gains volume overnight. The open landscape becomes only half-open again.

There is a theory based around a 'half-open landscape'. Our ancestors required from their environment the ability to both hunt and hide. This meant they needed open spaces (to prospect for food) and closed spaces (in which to hide from competitors). They evolved to favour half-open landscapes that provide both these opportunities in one place. I have no idea if this theory is true, but it makes sense to me and I think it is worthy of consideration if you happen to be designing a garden – certainly it is often in my mind. The hawthorn hedge along main avenue (when it is eventually planted) will leave a wide-open space running down into the valley on one side, but also frame and partition the garden on the other, making the progress from the house all the way to where the land falls away into the sky a truly half-open landscape.

In spring, I watch the mature hawthorn hedges we have already, noting their progress each day. Their leaves unfurl painfully slowly but then, suddenly, it has happened. They are back with a fullness that seems to cascade in layers down the side of the hedge. This is magnified not only by the additional hedging plants that I have put in (though they are still small) but also by the fact that I have allowed the existing hedges to grow larger. At this moment the leaves are a fresh, crisp green that knows no parallel, unsullied by sun, hail or wind. Soon they will sport little baubles of the purest white and when the hawthorn blossom finally opens it exudes a smell of summer leavened by salt, which hangs joyfully in the air. This smell is the guarantor that soon a new season will wrestle the old once again.

Hawthorn is my favourite of all hedging plants and I don't know why it isn't planted with more gusto by gardeners. It is also part of the rose family, and shows itself in that respect with its rude health and spiky impenetrable construction. It grows quickly. For these reasons it has always been favoured by farmers, which I suspect has given it an agricultural (rather than horticultural) feel in the eyes of the gardening public. But when you consider its blossom in spring, the peculiar green of its leaves in the summer and the bright red haws that adorn it all winter, it performs better than any other garden hedge. It can be kept relatively tight or allowed to romp. It supports more wildlife than any other native English plant save the oak, and it is far and away the best possible foil to the wind.

There is a well-worn country expression that gets lobbed around at dinner parties and social events during this pivotal moment of leaf break: 'Oak before ash and you are in for a splash; ash before oak and you are in for a soak.' I have never observed the ash tree break leaf before the oak, but at the other end of the year I have noticed how long oak trees can hold their leaves, with some here still in leaf on Christmas Day. Ash is almost the last of the trees to break leaf; poplars, maples, elms, oak and beech are all there first. Once the ash breaks you are home and dry; it is time to start thinking of planting out your tender vegetables and certainly the chance to do any work to the hedges has long passed.

It sounds like an obvious point to make, but a deciduous hedge is easier to cut when not in leaf because you can see what you are doing. I hate wearing gloves and leaves hide thorns, so for me cutting hedges in the winter results in fewer swingeing cuts to my hands and forearms. I have struggled with the hedges here. If I had a smaller garden with polite little stands of yew, privet and box, I could potter around at hedge-cutting time and probably not trouble with anything beyond a nice, light, battery-operated machine. It would be nothing but pleasure.

But twice a year, I have to really struggle; it is me against the hedges, and you will find me, often pirouetting, even with the long-handled hedge cutter, to reach some distant sprig; or crawling deep into a hedge fifteen feet wide to get at a central extrusion. This is my own fault. I have let the hedges here bulk out considerably from where they were when we arrived. Even as we enter our fourth growing season they are definitely not the hedges we bought. Why have I done this? Why have I doomed myself to a biannual contest between man and hedge? Quite simply: for leaf break. For a half-open landscape. For a place apart. So that as the fresh, clean green licks again through the hedges, Peverels lifts; it moves; it becomes hidden again.

One rose fades

My mother did it. She managed to keep going until baby Celestia was born, during our second autumn. Two days after her birth, Mum was driven up to Peverels by my middle brother and a nurse. She was in excruciating pain but she managed to cradle little Celestia in her arms. She also managed to compliment Sybilla and I on the home we had built; but soon she was tired. There was no question of showing her the garden.

The fact that I couldn't show her the garden and my plans for it outside was disappointing at the time, but the fact that neither of my parents have seen the garden matters less to me than I might have imagined it would. As I laid it out, I had moments of intense excitement that I would have deeply loved to share with them, but the basic sense of a place, that they would recognise, releases any pressure or pain in that regard. Once, my middle brother walked the garden with me and, musing, he said: 'I wonder what Daddy would have made of all of this then? I think he would have thought it rather eccentric, but I think he would have been pleased.' That was enough for me.

Anyway, my mother had done what she came for, a cuddle with Celestia, that was her nine-month target achieved. Now she had to return to London. Gingerly, we lifted her back into the car and rugged her up. Not for the first time, the image of a car driving away from me is seared into my memory alongside feelings of exquisite sadness and pain. It was the last proper time I spent with her, and at the time I knew it would be.

So this garden started all over again; a second time. I was nervous and waiting, separated by geography but trusting to some overarching sense of goodness. We had spoken on the phone and prayed together earlier in the day; entrusting her and everything to God. It had greatly comforted her. It had greatly comforted me. It seemed natural at the time. But my eldest brother had called to say things were now moving quickly again. My mother took her leave, three years and two days after my father had. In the middle of another grim January night. Both occasions were marked by terrible storms. Her funeral was held in the early spring in a church in London. It was a bright bold day and I returned to Peverels, aged thirty-three, an orphan.

Thirty-three is blessed, when you think of those who are orphaned in childhood, but then I think of my father-in-law whose mother was alive and well when he was well into his seventies. My mother managed to see all her children as adults, and to know six of her grandchildren, not a bad achievement.

A curious thing happened after my mother died, which was entirely unexpected. I was sad, and in pain, but I found within myself a new confidence, a new surety. That spring, just as my garden started out into its first true growing season under our stewardship, so my own sense of self-confidence seemed to rise with the sap. I found within myself a renewed commitment to living an authentic life, almost as if this were the only worldly good of any value. I remember laughing in among it too. Laughing would have been among my parents' instructions to me. An iteration of the well-worn phrase kept running through my mind: 'To lose one parent may be regarded as a misfortune; to lose both looks like carelessness.'

Bread doesn't bake itself and I had discussed my work situation with my mother. I knew that if I wanted to make my great garden project work, I would have to find some way of getting it to subsidise us. The decision to become a gardener and garden writer was still miles off. But I remember her central advice was to go where my talents lay; but this in no way automatically equated, in either of our minds, to being a garden writer. On the other hand, she had noticed my obsession and I remember her saying on one visit to her bedside in London, as I entered the room with thick wands of lavender and baskets of soft fruit, 'You really do like this gardening thing, don't you?' The expectation placed on my shoulders from my family wasn't relentlessly directed, but no one would have thought my job options might include writer, let alone garden writer. Regardless of the inherited assumptions, Sybilla had a vote too. She had been brave choosing me in the first place; could she be brave again backing me this second time while many of our friends were off working in business and earning ever-larger bonuses with all the lifestyle trimmings that accompany such things?

I can't remember whether I told my mother, or I just told myself (pain can make memory squidgy), that I would plant a tree in the meadow to remember her by. I think if I did tell

129

her, it was because I was casting around for something, anything, I could give; some effort at comfort, at further posterity. I haven't done it yet – there is still too much pain – but I will. In the meantime, my blue-eyed daughters remind me of my extravagantly beautiful and ruggedly tough mother.

Growing roses

Roses are part of a very important plant family called Rosaceae, which somewhat improbably includes many of the fruiting trees you will find in an ordinary English orchard, including such staples as apples, plums, pears and cherries. It is often said that if a rose could choose, it would choose clay soil. This is because they are hungry plants and while clay waterlogs easily and takes ages to warm up in the spring, its great saving grace is that it is packed with nutrients. The rose's hunger is also why you can't plant them where they have grown before unless you refresh the soil.

In most conditions, giving roses a thick mulch of well-rotted manure in the spring (a minimum of four inches) and a little liquid feed before their second flush of flowering is sufficient for their purposes and otherwise they require very little maintenance. You can make your own liquid feed from nettles and comfrey. I add some seaweed solution. Seaweed doesn't feed the plants; rather, it helps create a microbial environment within the soil in which the plants can feed as efficiently as possible. This law stands generally too: always try to feed the soil not the plant.

The good news is that roses (and for that matter buddleia, dogwood and willow) are among the easiest plants to take cuttings from, so increasing your stock at low cost is straightforward. I usually kill more cuttings than I keep, but with roses I have a solid success rate. You want to use a section of stem at least as thick as a pencil. With your secateurs make a flat cut just below a bud. Further up the cane make a slanting cut just above a bud so you remember which end should point up. You can place these cuttings into a nursery bed for transplanting the following summer, or even straight into the ground where you want them to grow. I use the latter method if I am taking a cutting on a whim. If you need to deter rabbits, dome some chicken wire over them in the flowerbed.

I have the most success when I use a terracotta pot filled with compost and horticultural potting grit, roughly half and half by volume. I slide the cuttings down into the mixture along the edge of the pot and then dress the top of the pot with potting grit, before placing them in a sheltered spot outside. While I generally prefer to use plastic pots in the garden (because they are water retentive and we garden in the driest part of Britain), I use terracotta pots for this precisely because they are porous and keep the compost from becoming sodden. Most cuttings are lost to rot. As I have learnt the hard way, leaf growth alone is no guarantee that the cutting has struck, merely that the race is on for sufficient roots to form to support further leaf growth. I never use rooting hormone and have plenty of success.

Few flowers hold such romantic power as roses, demonstrated by the fact that a handful rarely fails to raise a smile from my better half even when I am in the doghouse. I would grow them for tactical advantage on this basis alone. Roses are so versatile; when not scrambling up trees they can fill flowerbeds or break up boring lawns. They can make a part of the garden feel informal (when you let them romp) or formal if, for example, you grow them as standards. I think the old-fashioned approach, planting roses in vast beds all on their own, risks leaving them looking exposed. Roses seem to find themselves as they lose themselves. Isolate them and they lose the ability to sing.

Few plants are as subject to the changing whims of fashion and taste as the rose, and this has always been the case. Twenty minutes' drive north of Skymeadow is Kentwell Hall, a moated house, and a fine example of Elizabethan romance and splendour. I visited last summer and noticed the bridge over the moat is covered with a garish pink rose called American Pillar. It must be the remnant of a garden make-over undertaken at the beginning of the twentieth century. No one plants American Pillar now.

Vita Sackville-West declaimed the vulgarity of the American Pillar and also its common planting partner, Dorothy. In fact I like both, though they were probably overused in Vita's day. I grow Dorothy's offspring, Super Dorothy, as a weeping standard in the rose garden. It is very robust and has a graceful habit, though perhaps Vita thought the pink was veering towards Schiaparelli – it is certainly borderline. On the other hand, it is incredibly robust and over time will reach right down to the ground, creating the effect of a tea cosy of small flowers.

Another rose that has become unfashionable but I like very much is the Fairy. It is a low-growing shrub rose that is useful for ground cover and comes from a group called the Polyanthas, which were popular with the Victorians. Bowood House in Gloucestershire has two great box-edged beds of it immediately in front of the Adam Orangery. The Fairy starts into flower late, but its foliage is glossy and rich and certainly more than lovely enough to justify its presence in the border during the early part of the year. When it is in flower, it screams of the gentle civility of yesteryear and more or less defines prettiness. The fact that it is highly disease resistant secures its position in my lexicon of favourite roses.

Many modern roses are marketed as repeat flowering, though in reality what this means is that they tend to have one great flush, which starts in early summer, followed by a hiatus, and then a second flush, which starts in late summer and can continue well into autumn. Roses can come later still. I go out on New Year's Day to pick a vase of flowers for Sybilla. Every year it contains a rose or two.

As with many things in gardening, a certain amount of nonsense gets talked about what precisely is the right way to prune a rose, but the right time is certainly at the end of winter, unless you have climbers or any particularly exposed to the wind, in which case you should prune them in autumn to protect against wind rock. All my roses are pruned by the end of February, but if I lived in the north it might have to be put back to March. My view is that pruning too late is worse than too early. It is worth remembering, the earlier you prune, the earlier they will bloom, which of course stands to logic when you think about it. I have learnt that simply taking a pair of shears to them and cutting them to the shape you want is sufficient in most cases, and certainly for all the family of English roses that are so popular today.

The central fact about most roses is that they are robust. I cut an old rose to the ground one summer and forgot to return to dig its roots out. I was picking flowers from it that autumn. I remember fussing over a particular rose and then telling my mother about it on the telephone. She said to me with an unusual authority in her voice: 'Roses are tough. They have been around longer than you have!' She knew.

Berries

From late spring, berries start to pour in from the garden. At the weekend, the children and I often enjoy eating them for breakfast, usually in some combination of berries and yoghurt. I also grow rhubarb in the berry orchard and its long pink canes start off the season. You can force rhubarb by placing a pot over it but I don't bother; there is enough to do in the garden and I am content to eat it when the time comes. It requires rich soil and plenty of moisture. Most important of all, particularly with immature plants, is to remember not to harvest them at all in their first few years and thereafter to leave off harvesting until after June, in order that the plant can rest and use its leaves to store up goodness for the following season.

The first berries to roll in are, of course, gooseberries. Early gooseberries are sharp and late gooseberries remarkably sweet, so what I do is harvest every other berry early for a tart crop and return a few weeks later for a sweeter one. When my mother was ill I took her both in alternate batches. I derive comfort from the fact that I still have the very same bushes from which that particular harvest came, that I can touch them now as I touched them then, and look for a further harvest. It is a link. They feed us still. A tiny thing that for me holds a disproportionate significance. Though most of my gooseberry bushes have been moved many times, they thrive. Like roses, gooseberries are as tough as anything.

I can persuade the children to eat the first batch of tart gooseberries only if it is converted into a sweet, custard-rich fool. After these, it is the turn of the strawberries, raspberries, tayberries, blueberries and currants. One day, the mulberry tree I have planted will fruit too. Berries provide far and away the greatest eating bang for the least gardening buck, and I decided quite early on that I would dedicate a patch of ground immediately below the orchard to them. This area has become known as the berry orchard.

Berries generally do not mind being in part shade, which is lucky because the berry orchard is half shaded by the barn and protected to the north by a fifteen-foot-high run of laurel. I am convinced that because this garden is miles from anyone else's, and on the top of a hill, we have far less trouble from 'pests' and 'diseases' than the average garden, not that I intend to worry too much about pests and diseases in any case.

I am fed up with cultivated strawberries. Their flavour is so often all washed out. Instead, I now grow mainly wild straw-berries (sometimes called alpine or woodland strawberries). Wild strawberries are ever-bearing; they fruit all season long, but in lower quantities than their cultivated cousins. For this reason, you need to build up a very large stock of plants in order to guarantee a decent harvest at any one time. Every year, I start a batch from seed inside in seed trays. These get potted on, first into small pots and then into larger ones. If you try to skip straight into a larger pot I find they often dampen off (they wilt because there is too much water in the soil around their roots). As soon as they get pricked out of the seed trays they head out to the coldframes.

Each year I bring on fifty or a hundred plants from seed. They are slowly providing a ground cover in parts of the rose garden and within the snaking sweet-pea bed. Above all, wild strawberries actually taste of strawberry. In fact, one in four seem to taste exactly the way my daughter's strawberry crayons smell. There is nothing quite like experiencing this flavour with the just-smelt fragrance of a rose lingering in your olfactory network. I also grow a half-wild, half-cultivated form of strawberry called Mara des Bois. This variety is favoured by French chefs for its flavour, and shares a larger size with its cultivated cousins. I have a bed dedicated to them.

The other way of introducing strawberries to your garden is by buying them with dry roots. This is more expensive but more reliable and less bother than growing them from seed. You receive the plants in bundles and it is best to soak the roots in half a bucket of water before planting them. The technique for planting them is to make a hole in the soil and then mound earth in its centre like a little volcano. Rest the crown of the plant on the top of the volcano and spread the roots out down its sides. Then fill in with soil and water thoroughly.

When we arrived here there was a sunken bed for soft fruit down on the way to the meadow in what is now the miniature arboretum. In among it was a worthy clump of currants. I chose a couple of the best (white, black and red) and gave each one a good haircut before digging them up and moving

139

them to a bed that is now dedicated to currants in the berry orchard. White and red currants have a different pruning regime to blackcurrants but it is hard to tell them apart in winter, so I mark which is which.

The difference in pruning regime is purely down to the age of wood upon which the plant can be expected to fruit. Blackcurrants fruit on the previous season's wood, so you need to cut old stems right back to the ground each year, to encourage new growth and therefore more fruit in future years. On the other hand, red and white currants (and for that matter gooseberries and most apple trees) will fruit on older wood. So for these, you want to apply the goblet principle, in order to keep light and air flowing in. You can't get white currants in shops (except perhaps for very posh delicatessens in London, which I don't frequent), so I particularly like growing them in the garden and enjoy giving little punnets away to friends.

I also grow tayberries, blackberries and blueberries. The blueberries go in pots, so I can give them the acidic soil they like, but to me, nothing at all in the garden (even a pea fresh and sugary from the pod) rivals the complexity of flavour provided by a raspberry. There are two types of raspberry you can grow: summer fruiting and autumn fruiting. I have grown both, but I find the summer-fruiting varieties taste better so now these too have a dedicated bed in the berry orchard.

There is a pruning distinction here too, which, like all fruit pruning, turns on the age at which their wood will bear fruit. Summer-fruiting raspberries produce fruit on the previous season's growth. After harvesting in the summer, cut away all the old or weak canes, but keep the best canes from that season's growth for the following year's crop. You want thick sappy green ones. Tie them in. Autumn-fruiting raspberries, having a longer run, fruit on new wood that grows each season. So in February, you cut all the canes right back to ground level, and the new canes that emerge will bear your late autumnal fruit. As with all fruit, pruning hinges on light and air as well as the age of the wood upon which fruit will form.

The berry orchard is somewhat hidden; hidden by the laurel but also by the bulk of the house, the barn and even the cart lodge. Unlike much of the garden, subject as it is to the advance of the sky, the berry orchard is therefore an unusually sheltered spot, and an unusually good place to hide. Furthermore, in addition to extending the orchard, it causes us to visit that whole part of the garden for a larger share of the year than we would if the only bounty on offer were apples, pears and plums.

Gandalf's staff

In our third year, thinking about the six hundred and fifty feet of new hawthorn hedging still scheduled for planting in Skymeadow provided me with a lilting mixture of worry and excitement. Worry at the scale of the task (being a new project, it had to be done in addition to all the ongoing maintenance) and excitement because until it was done I knew I would feel a sort of anxiety about the garden. It would be sad (even hideous) if you couldn't enjoy a garden while building it. Besides, no garden, even when structurally complete, is in a sense ever finished.

On the other hand, a garden does achieve a sort of maturity once its core structure is in place. I was in a limbo of cruel expectation; anxious to meet my new garden in all its structural glory. It was a deep, desperate type of anxiety that kept me digging while others were inside with their feet up. Until the hawthorn hedge that was planned for main avenue was in, the last major structural piece of Skymeadow would be outstanding.

While my garden writing began to take off during our third year at Peverels, there was still a sense of risk before reward. I knew that all the hours (and pounds) I was pouring into the garden wouldn't be wasted, and would in some way be absolutely critical if I was to continue selling authentically garnered words on gardening, but nothing was definite, nothing was fixed; and the rate of expenditure seemed continually to outpace the relatively small sums generated from my article writing. This then was my risk capital; and from all angles it did look pretty risky. To be honest, I would have poured the same number of hours and pounds into the garden even in the absence of a financial plan, but that didn't change the fact that the chance of selling words was still my excuse for the expenditure.

I knew I couldn't let another season pass without getting the avenue and hedging in. But while I had chosen the variety of tree for the avenue, and I knew the hedge would be hawthorn, nothing would happen until I sat down and found someone to deliver the 750 whips (the same number of rabbit guards and canes) and the 16 somewhat unusual and quite expensive cherry trees. I toyed with the idea of not bothering with the rabbit guards (hawthorn is quite spiky) but we have a sufficiently virulent population in these parts that in my calculus the pain of losing multiple plants, after the effort of having put them in, made me reach for insurance.

My plan was for the new hedge to extend down the left-hand side of main avenue and branch off halfway along, obscuring Isaac's football pitch and providing a defined edge to the exotic orchard. As scheduled, it would be the final structural piece in Skymeadow and it would go in immediately after the avenue itself had gone in. I just felt that until the hedge was planted, the garden, taken as a whole, somehow hadn't 'happened'. I knew the fact of the hedging plants being small to start with wouldn't matter; the fact of their simply being there would. I knew that when it was in I would feel a sense of ease akin to the feeling I had after I sat my last finals exam at university. That evening I ate dinner and it just felt different. The little knot in my stomach had gone. Life was enjoyable again.

Still, I comforted myself with the progress that had been made. Within three years the rose garden could be said to have become established; the snaking sweet-pea border by the house, and all the other flowerbeds by the house, including the roundel for summer-flowering bulbs, were well established. The orchard had been expanded and brought back into proper order and now had a new border packed with roses, foxgloves and wallflowers. The pond was well on the way to becoming a bona fide wildlife garden. And the miniature arboretum now had new hedges, a gentle slope and a collection of interesting trees.

Furthermore, the vines in the exotic orchard were in, supported by a mixed planting of figs and a fig avenue. Innumerable trees, hedges and roses had been planted throughout the garden, and a settled strategy for the management of the different grass areas established. Paths had been created and vast numbers of pots and containers collected, planted and distributed around the garden with a diverse range of things growing in them from tulips through creeping thyme, to oak trees with a surround of marigolds, to tubs with toad lilies in shaded glades.

Even the vegetable garden, which had been moved each year (to the point where it became something of a joke between Sybilla and me), now seemed to have settled in its proper long-term location. Despite all this, until these last two elements were complete – the avenue and the hedge – the job felt categorically open. For no particularly good reason, at least not for one I understood, I had left the cornerstone to last.

Despite all this horticultural wizardry, despite the hard-won progress of those first few years, in among it all there was a point beyond which I could no longer put off opening my box; the little cardboard box I had been carrying around all my life into which I had placed all the difficult feelings; all the shards of myself I had thought I had lost, all the shards of others now gone. The box had been sitting under my bed and every time I looked at it, it seemed to shudder from side to side as if it contained a creature, a living thing. I needed to open it.

On a crisp spring morning – it might have been the morning after I returned from my mother's funeral – I decided the wait could go on no longer. I built up the courage and walked the box to the lawn, keeping my hand on the top so nothing would burst out and frighten me. Once the box was safely on the ground, surrounded and supported by all the progress in Skymeadow, I gingerly lifted the lid with a long stick. To my surprise out tumbled a little fledgling eagle with big bright yellow eyes and downy feathers. The box contained nothing else. It was otherwise completely empty.

I saw this fledgling little eagle; it was my grief; and I sensed rescue. I knew at that moment my fledgling grief needed sheltering, protecting, respecting, even feeding. My father had been a keen pilot, in his twenties throwing himself around north Essex in a Zlín aerobatic aircraft. The smell of aviation fuel reminds me of him, it almost is him. Still, when I hear the sound of a light aircraft, I smile; I feel his warm embrace, his joy and protection. I feel he is coming for me again. He took

146

me to the air when I needed him most. I remember wheeling around and floating, just me and him, defying gravity, defying the rules that other land-based people seemed to live by. His amusement as I whooped with excitement; as we made a tactical approach against an imagined enemy or chased a pigeon. My grandfather had been a pilot, too, in the Fleet Air Arm during the war. In my family, rescue always somehow came from the sky; I sensed some sort of rescue coming through my grief; through the little eagle.

Summer

A *summer harvest*

Summer is a time of harvest and last year we had a large one. By modern standards we live in a secluded spot, which brings many advantages; our sky is inky-black at night, there are no neighbours to be disturbed by the children's frequently high-pitched and high-volume play – or to complain when I let off fireworks – and no one need notice if one finds oneself mowing the lawn immodestly dressed! Of course, all these advantages bring with them their equal but opposite fact: we live in what is, by the standards of the south of England, a singularly isolated spot.

Sybilla and I are both in a sense ambitious about life generally, wanting to get on with things and always in a rush. But the flip side of this is that perhaps we lack caution. We have a tendency to throw ourselves straight into something with no (or perhaps very little) cold-headed calculation. Also, we had not reckoned on Sybilla's dyspraxia. Since taking this seriously we have learnt she has a relationship with the space around her that is just as profound, but ever so slightly different, to the rest of us. Understanding this began to make sense of a thousand little details in our lives; keys, phones, packing, tennis and even the need to have the surfaces in the kitchen clean and half tidy.

For the first eighteen months after we arrived at Peverels, across six driving tests and involving several increasingly frustrated driving instructors, we occupied a no-man's-land of hope, fear and uncertainty. Our assumption that Sybilla might need three months to get a driving licence, at the outside, had turned into six, six into nine and nine into eighteen. Sybilla had desperately wanted to secure her driving licence before my mother's demise, in order to bring Mum some pleasure and to ameliorate her worry, but that deadline too had sadly passed.

Everything, including being able to stay at Peverels, had been thrown into question and, worst of all, Sybilla would occasionally say, 'This whole thing is my fault.' Of course it wasn't.

I knew, whatever happened, I had to do my best to keep everyone calm and chipper. I kept bringing out the positives; how well the kids were doing, how well we were doing, and saying that I was happy to continue as family chauffeur for as long as it took, but we both knew that wasn't going to be possible for ever. The six school runs a day amounted to three hours a day behind the wheel. It was frankly disorientating and I remember at the end of the spring term beginning to feel dizzy when I looked at the car, which as someone who has always been happy to drive merely for pleasure was novel. During that period I developed a deep admiration for the nation of parents (mostly mothers) who do the school run.

On the positive side, the countryside is, ironically, so much less anonymous than a city. In a city there are people all about and because of this they don't feel such a need to mingle. People will live for twenty years in a flat not knowing the people in the flat above. On the other hand, the geography of the country inclines people towards community life. We were massively supported by a small network of kind neighbours who went out of their way to step in when our logistical system periodically ground to a halt. We will be forever grateful.

Sybilla was nervous before every single driving test, feeling the full force of responsibility for our home and future increasingly weighing on her. Someone, probably my mother, had suggested rescue remedy, which is an herbal distillation with an alcohol base, for calmness. On our innumerable drives to the test centre, pipette after pipette got squirted feverishly into the mouth until I had to point out that if she carried on she might find that she was over the limit. After her sixth test, just before she went into labour with Celestia, I had talked to the examiner and he said to me, 'She is not far off now.' It was a small word of encouragement but we both really needed it.

We know now that dyspraxia does not mean you can't drive: it just means it takes you a lot longer to learn how to drive than someone who is not dyspraxic. In fact, I think that a dyspraxic's brain has to compensate to learn these skills to such an extent that, when they are eventually learnt, they are learnt better and more thoroughly than a non-dyspraxic. But during that eighteen-month slog it felt like there were no guarantees.

Looking back on this whole period, we can see we found a new level of shared reliance and mutual respect for each other; a true summer harvest. But hindsight is a wonderful thing: when you are in the furnace it doesn't always feel like you are being refined by it.

On her seventh attempt, on the seventh day of the seventh month, Sybilla's efforts came to fruition. I had tried, several instructors had tried, but in the end Sue, a specialist at teaching people with dyspraxia, helped Sybilla get to the point where she could get herself over the line. As she drove into the station car park in Clacton, where Isaac, Celestia and I waited, not daring to believe it might be the moment of deliverance, Sue asked her, 'So, shall we pretend to your husband that you failed?' Sybilla answered quick as a flash: 'That man has been through enough with my driving. There is no way I am stringing this out for a moment longer than necessary.'

As she turned the corner into the car park I stole a glance through the windscreen and saw her thumb was up. I leapt out of the car, kicked my feet, jumped as high as I have ever jumped and let out a howl of delight. I don't often, but on that occasion I blubbed. So did she. We had done it. We could stay in the home and garden of our dreams. All the time, the commuters at Clacton railway station looked on, somewhat bemused.

For months after, every morning was a celebration. We would both wake up and pinch ourselves. We took simple pleasure in her being able to say, nonchalantly, that she might just pop over and see so and so, or drop down to the shop for a bottle of milk. These experiences were new, and rich and life-giving. Sybilla said she felt that she had finally grown up. However hard the road had been, now we were at the summit it yielded so much more than we could have expected. In a funny way, it felt like more than just a driving licence. It felt a bit like a threshold for both of us; somehow akin to moving from childhood into adulthood, the final piece of the puzzle. We had a settled home, a family and we also had a puppy. We just had to figure out how I would make a living.

Sybilla had survived eighteen months living in an isolated farmhouse with four children and no driving licence; through a pregnancy and, often, carrying a grieving husband. But in this moment of triumph we didn't forget the host of supporters who would be celebrating this one atop a cloud, cracking open the heavenly bubbles. We thought of Sybilla's amazing granny Rara, who we all loved so much, and of both my parents. They had all loved us and loved our kids. They had all been there for us when we needed them. Importantly, they had all been tough, but they had sheltered us when we needed sheltering. They weren't here now, of course, but they were somehow caught up in this celebration. They had all paid into the Charlie and Sybilla enterprise one way or another, and this was their day too.

Lost to a green cathedral

To be happily lost, and to be at home, is a fine thing. On a summer's morning, as I swing open the heavy oak door of my study, I have this sense of stepping out into a green cathedral and the first thing I am conscious of, as I place my bare foot upon the rich and verdant grass, is its intricate floor, composed not just of grass, but of other escapees and vaga-bonds. From the moment the wild violets emerge in spring, this motley sward never ceases to surprise or delight; packed as it is with a generous showing of wild herbs, thistles and what would commonly be thought of as weeds.

The glut of wild violets in the spring, massed through swathes of lawn, provide a hauntingly beautiful spectacle, particularly if you bother to get down to their level. Wild violets are so delicate they make my stomach quiver and my legs tingle. I have always preferred delicate violas to garish pansies, but the crowning glory of this type, to my mind, is the wild pansy, known traditionally as 'heartsease'. I wish it would spread itself around here but, despite being a native in some parts of Britain, to date it has been reluctant. In the meantime, I grow a dedicated pot of it on the table outside our kitchen.

Every year, despite being exiled in north Essex, the Californian poppies seem to come sooner. The ones down in the rose garden wait for the sun to crest the great elm hedge before recommencing their daily sway westward, but they have long escaped the confines of the rose garden and pop up where they are least expected; not in the sward itself but at its margins, providing a bejewelled edging. The colour is a burnished orange-gold, like a miniature sun, as vibrant as any colour I know in nature, or any colour that was ever painted on the stonework of a pre-Reformation cathedral. At night they tuck themselves up and look almost mournful.

Californian poppies (and opium poppies, but not oriental poppies) are self-seeding annuals. They grow, flower, set seed and die in a single season, but once introduced they will return each year in self-sustaining little colonies and often in pleasing places, but my struggle is weeding them out of places where I don't want them. In this sense, they are anti-structural. Or more accurately, Arcadian, in the way in which they lose themselves, creating chaos and variety within the overall structure of the garden.

My most exciting self-seeding episode here to date, and my greatest unintentional victory in the garden, happened in the miniature arboretum just to the north of the rose garden. I had used the old soft-fruit area there for a mishmash of things (like a dishevelled nursery bed) and it included a few clumps of oriental poppies. The soft-fruit area had been sunken into the ground and the spoil mounted round the sides, presumably to provide shelter. Further down was a bonfire area that had also been dug out. The ground was effectively trenched and ridged in all the wrong places (for my purposes) and I wanted to restore an even natural slope. I considered doing it by hand but even I baulked at the prospect, so a friend brought his mini-digger up for the day. There is a definite skill to using a mini-digger efficiently and it is one I do not possess. However, I did have a go and using a joystick to effortlessly pull through yards of soil at a time was, to one so accustomed to a spade, a sort of ecstasy.

We levelled the area in the autumn. Afterwards, we spread grass seed on the bare earth and stamped it in together as a family. It was good fun. In the following few weeks, I was incredibly busy with work commitments and it was unseasonably dry. I kept worrying that I hadn't got a hose down there for the grass seed, but as it turned out it was lucky I hadn't. The next spring, just as I was preparing to start mowing the area in order to bring it into the same regime as the neighbouring areas of grassland, I saw thousands upon thousands of oriental poppies coming up across a vast area, about the size of a tennis court.

The seeds had come from the oriental poppies in the old soft-fruit area and when we levelled it we had inadvertently also spread the seed around remarkably evenly. I weeded all around the oriental poppies, mostly removing the grass we had sown the previous autumn, and some mustard and jumping jack that had spotted the opportunity and were moving in from below the hedge. That summer we had an extravagant and, I think, audacious oriental poppy field. It is a fertile spot and they grew well above my head, so we cut a maze into it and the children enjoyed rushing about, lost among the blowsy peaches, purples and crimsons. This is the sort of fun that can be had with plants that will reliably lose themselves.

As well as poppies, other solid self-seeders include forget-me-nots, linarias, aquilegias (all of which unsurprisingly have rugged native British meadow or woodland pedigrees) and also love-in-a-mist and hollyhocks. I manage the grass carefully, with strips of meadow that rise almost to the house. Some is cut only once a year at the end of the summer; other patches get a second cut in early spring but are then left. These are the patches that the bee orchids seem to favour. Careful management has already brought the bee orchids back in droves and I can count fifty or sixty in a single walk. The purple bee orchid is a lovely thing, but last year I saw the less common white bee orchid. It didn't come back this summer, but that is the way with orchids. They won't be forced, only gently teased.

In addition, Skymeadow is littered with bird's-foot trefoil, known to country folk as anything from granny's toenails to butter-and-eggs. I love the old common names; they survive precisely because they have been tested by time to perfection. It forms clumps of bright yellow. Vetch, too, likes our soil and leaves the grass shot through with magenta sparkles. Both flowers are legumes and have that delicate orchid-like flower typical of the pea family. Much of our soil is rich, too rich for a traditional wildflower meadow set-up. But I like it that way and, in fact, I stand against the conventional approach to managing a wildflower meadow, by leaving the mown and mulched grass where it falls. By doing this I have been rewarded with great arching grasses that rise well beyond my height, and make a maze of extensive tranches of the meadow.

Every time you mow you renew a covenant with the grass, the importance of which is incalculable. By mowing you are favouring grass over woodland, and grass is the cornerstone for so much more human achievement than is generally reckoned. Grass outcompeted woodland originally through its ability to recover quickly from mowing (original mowing was, of course, undertaken by either grazing animals or greedy wildfire). From this genesis early men and women realised they could use grass (including corn and barley) not just for bread, but also to feed their animals during the leaner months. Almost everything we eat is a result of converting grass, in one way or another, into calories. Almost all farming is managing this process; we owe grass an awful lot.

In spring, when the grass raises its first, fresh green growth of the year and you feel as though you can almost see it growing, the sudden roll of green across the landscape is primordially exciting. Apes, apparently, have nerves for blue and red light reception while humans have a third receptor for green. There is a theory that the development of this third receptor gave us an evolutionary advantage for recognising and working with grass, and for grading its quality. We are hardwired to extract pleasure from the green shades of nature. I need them like I need water.

In addition to its intricate floor, our cathedral has heavily buttressed walls and a nave. Along the drive there are seven monstrously large Lombardy poplars, each a good seventy-foot tall. They are fastigiate trees (which means they grow narrowly, a bit like a pencil). They can be seen from several miles away and when we turn the corner and they hove into view, my children have come to traditionally shout 'poplars to Peverels' as quickly and as loudly as they can.

This part of Essex is famous for its Lombardy poplars because the Courtaulds, a family of local landowners, planted them with gusto. Pencil-like on the horizon, the trees give the view over the valley, particularly under a baking midsummer sun, a Tuscan feel. The poplars on our drive were planted before the war by a small girl called Margaret and her father.

161

We met Margaret when we first arrived here – she lived in an old people's home down the valley but still worshipped, every Sunday, come rain or shine, in the village church. Her nephew (himself in his seventies) brought her up to Peverels regularly so she did not lose her link with the landscape she had known intimately for almost a century.

After the poplars, the drive opens into a space enclosed by tall hedging, which houses a small orchard with a cart lodge on one side and an old Essex barn on the other. The drive slightly oddly then proceeds right past the house (as if it were oblivious to it) and slap-bang through the centre of what we call the home garden before stopping, somewhat abruptly and inexplicably, below the great elm hedge. When we first arrived at Peverels, part of me resented this path. I considered scrubbing it out and imposing a new, more classical order on the space that runs away from the house down the valley, possibly even filling in the duck pond to achieve some symmetry, but I never felt comfortable deep down about doing this. I needed to listen to this path – I knew it had a purpose.

I am grateful I stayed my hand because over time I came to see this path for what it was – a metaphorical river, a nave, that runs through Peverels as a central axis along which all the garden rooms that make up the cathedral now sit. But it couldn't stop just below the elm hedge as if artificially dammed; it needed to carry on out into the meadow.

So we continued this metaphorical river into the meadow, and it became an avenue, it gained order, it became more nave-like. It stretched and it marched all the way to our boundary, all the way to the place where the land drops away dramatically into the valley below, giving the sense that the avenue seems to flow out beyond our boundary and on into the eternity of the sky.

This point of meeting, where the finite seems to touch the infinite, where land and sky meet, is our green cathedral's altar. It is the place where all the organising energy of the garden submits itself to the sky. I started a cairn at this point, like the ones you might see in Scotland, a collection of the very best stones I find as I dig, heaped in no particular order, one upon the other. People have brought stones to add. A friend brought one from the tiny island of Lindisfarne. It marks the ancient seventh-century journey of Saint Cedd, who arrived from Lindisfarne and carried the gospel up the river estuaries of the Colne and Stour. It sits at the top.

Here, there is a gospel; it is a gospel of surrender, a ceding of control, where the garden itself surrenders to the impetus of the sky; to the fact of an eternity beyond its control. My grief, eagle-like, rushes down this avenue. I follow the garden and the eagle willingly into this point of surrender, to a place where no anxious thought can ultimately prevail, to a point beyond the harrow. To a place where it is possible to be idle and free; to be both lost and found.

Looking up

Our cathedral is tied to the sky every bit as much as the great cathedral at Ely is tied to its roof. But our roof changes through the seasons, every day, by the minute. It is solid only when entirely obscured or entirely clear. Every year, what I call the 'first really good day' goes into my gardening diary. There is no strict definition of what the first really good day looks like, but I always know when I have just had it. But, unlike bright and beautiful spring days, when clouds scud across the sky, the first really good day must have a solid roof; bright and solidly blue.

A solid roof, together with noticeable heat, creates the feeling of summer. Warm underfoot in the morning and cloudless from dawn until dusk, the panoply of gifts brought by a summer sky. This year, the first really good day was 5 May. In the morning, I drove down to Sussex for an event at which

I was speaking. It was 12°C at eight in the morning and then in the twenties all day. After Sussex I was off up to London for another event at which I had to speak. The sky was cloudless all day. The car hot and sticky. Summer.

It sounds like an odd thing to say, but if you want to have a relationship with the sky you need to live near it. People often choose to live by the sea and your proximity to the sea can be measured in a line from Towcester (which I was always told was in the centre of England) to the coast, via where you live. But living beside the sky is not an entirely different matter; it is plain that someone in a house will have a different relationship to the sky versus someone who lives on the top floor of a skyscraper. But the difference works at a more basic level too, driven by topography. Skymeadow is about as close to the sky as you can get; a cosy cottage etched into the rock of a steep valley isn't. There is no right or wrong, but I doubt many people consider what they like in this regard before they buy a house.

It is a fact, however, that if you want views, you must live on a hill, which means in the sky. If you live on a hill you must suffer wind. Despite this, having lived on a hill, I don't think I would ever wish to exchange it for a sheltered pocket of a valley. But hills have their drawbacks too. You can't hide on a hill and the level of exposure to the elements you face can be withering. It forces a type of emotional honesty. It can be uncomfortable. I think people respond to the houses and places in which they live; I think it moulds them more than they dare admit. I have seen this with friends of mine whose various epochs have been oddly related to the feel of the house and place in which they happened to live at the time. It is why you shouldn't put your prime minister in a palace if you want them to remain humble. It is why Versailles wasn't such a great idea after all. It is why an impoverished physical environment will lead to an impoverished emotional one. It is why I want to live next to the sky.

The eastern seaboard of the UK tends to have less light pollution than the rest of the country because of the low population (relatively speaking), combined with the dark grey swell of the North Sea. This is stargazing country and the inky-black night sky lends itself to the shrieks of delight as our friends from cities see a shooting star. They shriek, too, merely at the scale of the heavens above. I think the influence of the North Sea must also be why the light in East Anglia seems to have a different quality to the light in other parts of the country. Not necessarily better, just different. It is somehow lighter light. As if it were a strain of light that might, somehow, have just a little less mass.

The sky is a fact of our existence. In high summer the sun sets over the far corner of Skymeadow, dipping down below the reservoir. We often walk out to the cairn at the end of main avenue to bid it farewell. Each of my children has a sense of the rising and setting of the sun that is indelibly tied to the sky under which we live. We look into the sky for planets. We look into the sky for dreams and ideas. We look into the sky together. Venus, the bright morning star, glows bright. Our lives together are fashioned by how close we are to the sky every bit as much as they would be if we lived next to the sea.

Birdsong is truly the sound of early summer and it too seems to come from the sky. I long for it all through the dark days. Sometimes the birdsong here becomes so overwhelming that it could make a fevered mind crazy, just as the sound of the wind on the Atlantic coast can. Obsessing over a garden could make a fevered mind crazy, too. The sky has its own commentary on madness, in all its various forms. G. K. Chesterton wrote: 'The poet only asks to get his head into the

167

heavens. It is the logician who seeks to get the heavens into his head. And it is his head that splits.' The fevered, anxious mind is not illogical but only logical.

Fevered anxiety is logic with nothing else; logic unbalanced by the random happenstance of life; logic without poetry; logic without family; logic that has become ugly and egotistical; logic that is separated from the human heart; that has been cut free from the human family it should rightfully serve; logic without the sky; a movement of the soul that looks only down and never up. Othello's jealousy was as logical as it was disconnected from the truth. Like Othello's jealousy, logic let loose will feed upon that which it consumes. Wars are usually started quite logically, but have always been won either in the sky or through reference to it. High ground is sky ground. Logic has its place, it is beautiful in its way, but let out into all places it will soon run amok. Logic is a servant not a master; invert this and it becomes a very blunt instrument indeed.

And yet, gardening is a place where poetry and logic commingle with a sort of inescapable indivisibility. Gardening is a science unquestionably; plants are classified and their growth follows the hard penumbra of a series of equations as surely as the trajectory of an Exocet missile. Any plantswoman or plantsman knows this. But, this is important only because it isn't. In the end, I garden merely to get a glimpse of the heavens. The attempt to catch everything within the controllable confines of logic is a path to raging anxiety. The garden doesn't fundamentally need me. I am there only as a fortunate, grateful, onlooker and tinkerer, questing for glimpses of beauty and hope. Logic must surrender. Poetry is to be found in this surrender; to me poetry is this surrender.

Birdsong reminds me of this. Looking up reminds me of this. The eagle reminds me of this. It is perspective, it is sky knowledge; it keeps me on the right side of the tracks. I think we need this knowledge in the garden; I think we need it as we build our careers; I think we need it most of all as we grieve. Logic didn't help me grieve, but the gratitude born of unconditional surrender did. I see this clearly in the vastness of the heavens. I see it every time I look up.

Nightingales and orchids

I used to go hunting orchids with my father in June, and now I take my children. It is as exciting a quarry as any other and I recommend it to anyone who lives near some accessible countryside or woodland. Also in June, my father and I would sometimes get into the Land Rover and go to the gravel pits outside Long Melford to listen for nightingales. When we got there he would turn the lights off, open the windows and light his pipe. If I tried to talk he would hush at me. When friends came to stay we would sometimes take them with us.

I heard a nightingale in Skymeadow last summer. They are an ordinary-looking bird, a little like a blackbird, and they like hedges and shrubs. Fortunately we have no shortage of either. By July they have all gone – June is the month of nightingales and orchids. It is extraordinary to think that we can still hear the very same song Shakespeare did. But what if one year they didn't come back?

My father was one of the first people in our area to convert our farm to an organic operation. I remember the process well. In fact, even before conversion he had run a very wild-life-friendly operation. One thing he had always done was to leave wide verges (wide enough to drive on) around the edges of all the fields at home. While this was commercially nonsensical it radically improved conditions for both insects and the birds that ate them. This is why he did it. He loved the whole of creation in all its wonder and wisdom, and he wanted more not less of it. This yearning for abundance and diversity is locked into the DNA of organic practice.

Our industrial use of herbicides and pesticides in Britain since the war has swished through our insect populations like a giant scimitar. Over the last fifty years some have been halved, quartered and then halved again. Two species of bumblebee have become extinct in Britain already, but this is just the tip of the iceberg. The real test comes from talking to people who drove cars in the 1960s. They all remember that a short journey in high summer would leave their windscreens thick with bugs. This never happens now and I don't believe it is entirely down to more aerodynamic automobile design. I have noticed this even over the course of my fifteen years of driving; I used to have to wipe the bugs off, and I rarely do now.

So far, I have managed to run an entirely organic operation here. When we moved from London I brought some rose spray with me. I went out one day to spray the roses and just thought to myself, *Why am I doing this?* Since then we haven't touched a single chemical. Nothing. Einstein reputedly said that if bees became extinct he would give the human race four years. I garden organically principally because I want to play no part in the ongoing decimation of our insect populations and I want this little seven-acre island, surrounded by conventionally farmed land, to become a wildlife haven.

Of course, I also want to grow healthy plants, so I am trying to encourage a balanced ecosystem. Seeking this balance is deeply satisfying. Birds, which for example eat the slugs and snails that will otherwise eat my plants, are an important part of this process. But so is lavender and rosemary, the principal home for overwintering ladybirds who eat the aphids on my roses. The ones they miss get squished by Sybilla and me, often on a summer's evening, often with a glass of wine in hand.

I now have seven bird-feeding stations around the house to keep my pest-control team well nourished. Each is positioned to be clearly visible from one of the ground-floor rooms; they bring us great pleasure. From the first frost I put the peanut feeders out. Peanuts are high in energy and a good winter food for songbirds. There are only two rules – don't give them mouldy peanuts from disreputable suppliers (as they can be poisonous) and, particularly during the spring breeding season, only ever feed peanuts through a wire mesh as whole ones can choke fledglings.

My favourite of all the little birds who visit our feeders are the long-tailed tits. They look like somewhat scruffy flying table-tennis balls. As they argue with the blue tits, chaffinches and robins for control of the feeders, scraps of peanut or lard tumble onto the gravel below and provide welcome sustenance to the dunnocks, ground-feeding songbirds with tiger stripes across their brown backs. No food is wasted. A single blue tit or long-tailed tit at the bird table usually indicates a tribe of fifteen or twenty waiting off in the nearest bush for their turn.

Hedges are effectively highways for wildlife, and the large hedge along the north of Skymeadow runs down into the bottom of the valley, creating access between the valley basin and our garden for both birds and insects. I have let many of our hedges grow taller in order to provide additional shelter, but I am also careful about when I cut them and I sacrifice a neat garden in order to leave berries and haws in place through the winter months as an additional food source. Naturally, I also avoid disturbing the hedges during the spring breeding season.

I apply the same theory to the flowerbeds now too and never clear them up until spring. This greatly increases the ready availability of seeds, berries and insects as a food source for birds during the winter months; it also looks better. In addition to providing feeders (and enough of them to mitigate the risk of disease spreading between birds), I also make sure they have sheltered perching spots near their feeders because birds like to move from safety to food and back again. As a result of all this, I believe we have a vastly larger songbird population than when we arrived. During the spring their song becomes noticeable at dusk and then eventually reaches a fever pitch of excitement. If you stand in the courtyard it can be almost deafening. This all makes me very happy.

People often reach for non-organic solutions to problems because they seem easy; what could be easier than spending thirty minutes spraying the roses? But it is so short-sighted. What could be better than growing healthy roses that don't need spraying each year? Similarly, by encouraging insects, and their predators, the steps you need to take to address both diminish rather than increase. Healthy plants in healthy soil are far less prone to disease. Why spread a deathly rug over the microbes in your soil and then watch your plants ail, each season needing more intervention than the last? It is barmy when you think of it, but it has made a whole new industry based on short-term intervention and that, of course, is good for business. The true economy of organic gardening runs in the right direction; a little more effort today leads to a lot less effort tomorrow; this is so often true inside, why then do we doubt its efficacy outside? If we wish for June to be the month of nightingales and orchids, if we wish to preserve the trousseau of creation for each generation, if we wish for our grandchildren to continue to hear the song Shakespeare did, we will have to address our approach to stewardship.

A *new confidence*

As recounted, a curious by-product of the grief I felt after losing my mother was a mounting confidence; it had come with the eagle, and it mounted in our second summer. It grew as the eagle grew. A newly planted tree will often spend a season or two languishing, sulking after the move and starting the process of creating a new anchorage, but then suddenly the sulk is over, the anchor is down and growth rapidly takes off. It is that sudden start into growth, real growth, that filled me with hope that summer.

On the one hand, I could see the rose garden beginning to do the things to the rest of the garden that I had intended for it to do. It was growing into the beating heart of the garden, and I could see a certain fulfilment to the original vision. To be sure, the rose garden was far from what gardeners call established, but its promise was now beyond doubt.

On the other hand, I could see that, shorn of parents, one is also in some vague sense shorn of excuses. When you no longer have parents, there is no one to blame if you choose to live in a way that isn't authentic. When the king is dead, you become the king. The buck stops with you.

A garden that wasn't, transforming gently into a garden that is, can provide a rock-like foundation for hope, and a king that wasn't, transforming gently into a king that is, can too. It is still on balance better not to lose one's parents (there is nothing wrong with being a princess or a prince) but nature abhors a vacuum and I found that as one thing was taken, something else was given; my grief had become a gift; a beautiful soaring eagle. I found freedom and I found responsibility, including the responsibility that knows it can err and fail, and I felt these things run through my fingers, like a knotted rope that was mine to hold and pull and fashion. It was a pleasing feeling.

I found that there is strength and hope; this I found simply because there is strength and hope. But the change in my finding it was subtler still; now, the strength and hope I found was found directly. It was felt directly. I no longer needed an interlocutor. I no longer had an interlocutor. I was the interlocutor. The crown had been elsewhere, but in some dimly understood way, it was now on my head. There is something about the unbroken chain from oak to oak or queen to queen or king to king. There are beautifully embroidered gloves to be worn in each generation; there is shade and protection to be provided in each generation; there is a sword to be grasped in each generation.

All of this filled me to overflowing with a sense of authenticity and this authenticity bubbled out of my soul like a strong river and washed away the fear and compromise of yesteryear. It set my course, and it has been grinding through

178

the rocky obstacles it has found ever since. I felt at last that I could see this river; I could see it with unblinking eyes, without flinching; for that is what the eagle does. So the eagle and I explored the river, all its eddies and turns; and I learnt to watch it calmly, like the eagle. From truth everything else flows. Without truth there is nothing. I haven't turned my back on the 'sensible' life that might have been chosen for me by parent or peer, but that summer I engaged with the river in a way that I had never done before. I accepted it. I found it was our river; it belonged to the eagle and myself. I explored it fully and have been doing so ever since. And all this led to a number of exciting work developments.

By our second summer I had started to drive my tanks onto the lawn. Through dispatching numerous emails to invisible editors, I had started to have the odd piece accepted. To others, including Sybilla, this could have still all amounted to no more than a hobby, a break before real work recommenced. But I knew it was more than that. I knew it was intentional. I knew it was a start. As I put about the fact that I was interested in gardening and was open for business, either writing about gardens or helping people with their own, things started to gain momentum. I started trading on this idea in thought and conversation.

I remember my brother saying that no one in our family had ever done something like this before; but why not? I was breaking cover. The bubble of an idea was sitting atop my outreached trowel. But I knew that if I was selling words I needed many more transactions for their delivery, and if I was selling garden schemes I needed a richer seam of clientele. All in all, I knew I needed some sort of break. I remember thinking that somehow wangling my way into something like the Chelsea Flower Show might be helpful, but while I had made a small start, there was no obvious way of converting it into something that might cut the mustard at the world's premier horticultural show.

Still, as my inner confidence grew, the garden grew too and was like a sacrament, the outward manifestation of an inwardly felt grace. All the best things in life are sacramental, and they are all felt for the first time with an indescribable newness and wonder. Life is sacramental, marriage is sacramental, new life is sacramental and the journey each of us makes towards our own attempt at being a responsible monarch also seems to me to carry something sacramental to it. We are each handed swords of justice, mercy and truth. My grief taught me that we each have a coronation. We are each of us capable of both rational and just action, we are wondrous creatures standing somewhere in a chain of command that stretches back to time immemorial.

Cottage garden

July is the month when everything groans with fruit and flower. It is the moment before the flatness of August, before the garden collapses in exhaustion. It is the moment when a cottage garden can be at its fullest and most frenzied. The most appealing aspect of a cottage garden, to me at least, is its concept of efficiency; not something most people associate with cottage gardens. But while 'cottage garden' has come to mean a style of gardening that is all pastel and picket, the origin of cottage gardening is much more interesting than that.

In the eighteenth and nineteenth centuries the great estates, helped by Brown, developed an entirely new way of thinking about the outdoors. Previously, nature had been something to be dominated and mastered. Out of this came the neat, managed spaces of France, almost like indoors outside. We had them here too, and a few survive. But Brown swept all this away and attempted instead to capture the essential glory of the English countryside, though still in a managed way. He painted pastorally using trees, lakes and contours as his palette. Out of this grew the concept of Arcadia; spaces that were in some senses organised but contained within them a pleasing, natural, anarchy. Often Brown had to move cottages in order to clear views.

But, during this same period, those very same cottagers had to manage a certain reality on one side and a pressure on the other. On the one hand, they needed outside space to grow vegetables and herbs. On the other, they had to demonstrate an aesthetic that kept the people in the big house happy, that sat comfortably within the new concept of a distinctly English Arcadia. The cottage garden resolved this tension. It ensured that every scrap of space was used; first for supplemental food, then for the herbs necessary to flavour and treat ailments, and finally, where possible, for flowers to adorn. Of course, where crossover existed (for example a vegetable, herb or fruit that was also decorative) so much the better. The cottage garden, like the great park, was a sort of Arcadia; chaos within an ordered (and clearly delineated) boundary. From this flows the sense of ease, and of efficiency, that pleases me in a cottage garden. The pastel and picket aesthetic marketed on the back of seed packets is a by-product.

My ambition is for the area around the house slowly to grow into a cottage garden, or at least in places to resemble half a cottage garden. However, I am resigned to the fact that with all the other developments in Skymeadow that are scheduled, this will take time. Nonetheless, this year I have a new flowerbed near the house in our 'cottage garden' area. It is devoted to summer-flowering bulbs and rhizomes. I am particularly excited about the irises. The soil in the new bed is better than anywhere else in the garden (brown and crumbly and plenty of it above the clay) so there must have been a stable or a sty there at some point in the past.

A friend of mine runs a plant nursery down the road and he is bringing on a few of the Cedric Morris irises that have recently been rediscovered. Sir Cedric Morris was a famous artist who set up an art school in Suffolk during the 1930s. He viewed gardening as an extension of his painting and he bred new strains of iris. Most were lost, but the heroic efforts of a small team led by a former head gardener at Sissinghurst has led to their rediscovery. They literally went searching for forgotten clumps of them in people's front gardens in Suffolk. I have C. Morris Benton and C. Morris Susan on order from my friend.

The Cedric Morris irises are part of the large summer-flowering group of irises that you would associate as equally with a grand herbaceous border as a cottage garden. Their flowers are good for cutting, which gives them solid cottage-garden status. A cottage garden was a cut-flower patch in addition to a herbarium and a collection of fruit and veg. These large irises can be bearded (with fleshy hairs on their falls) or less commonly beardless (smooth falls), and they grow from rhizomes. The rhizomes of my bearded irises look like langoustines, and should be planted with their tails pointing southwest and protruding from the soil so they can bake in the sun.

These large summer-flowering irises are not to be confused with the smaller *Iris reticulata* family. *Reticulata* irises grow from bulbs (as opposed to rhizomes) and flower very early in the spring, alongside snowdrops. Two popular ones, for example, are Harmony and Katharine Hodgkin. These small early flowering irises are a joy in an otherwise spartan garden and perfect for putting in pots to deliver spring colour inside or out.

Clematis is another plant that can deliver pleasing sprawl to a cottage-garden scheme. I grew a clematis in London called Parisienne, which provided flowers in a very appealing blue from May through to October. As with many plants it was bought initially for the romance of the name. Sybilla lived in Paris for six months when we were stepping out together. When we moved here I inherited a number of clematis, but the one that stands out is John Paul II, which grows over two obelisks behind a fence and provides a fabulous summer display of large pure white flowers. I suspect John Paul II was bought by my predecessor for the name too.

The clematis I most wanted when we moved here was one called *Clematis cirrhosa*. To be sure, this is not a plant likely to attract sales on account of its name, but it does give away the fact that the flowers are exotically 'freckled'. I have two stands of it growing up high obelisks in the rose garden, where they provide a welcome lift in January, and get on with their clematis-like life for the rest of the year.

Clematis can be very confusing for the uninitiated (certainly they were for me), principally because they fall into three separate pruning groups. But this is less complicated than it seems at first glance. It all hinges on when they flower. Those in pruning group 1 flower early (like the *cirrhosa* varieties, or the ubiquitous Montana), and should be pruned lightly if at all immediately after flowering. Those in group 2 flower in midsummer (for example John Paul II), and can be given a light prune after flowering, with a more substantive one the following February. Finally, those that flower late in the year, group 3, should be given a prune in February. Theory is all very well, but in practice the rules can be simplified further: group 1 get little or no pruning until they start growing where you don't want them; the rest get relatively stern treatment in February. So far, this is working for me.

I am lucky that my parents-in-law love gardens almost as much as I do. My mother-in-law has an unusual talent for pots and Sybilla's grandfather was an accomplished gardener, or at least garden owner. He had several acres of market garden and a famous herbaceous border, so my father-in-law is usually the repository of sound gardening advice. I struggled with the solution to two dense and tangled clumps of clematis that were here when we arrived. I decided to only lightly prune them in the hope this would cause them to spill over the fence behind which they are planted. In retrospect, I made an error. So last year I pruned them hard in February and as usual gave them a trowel full of fish blood and bone and a mulch of compost. They rewarded me with the best display yet. As my father-in-law often says: so often the answer is to cut harder than you dare.

Font

Particularly if you don't have any already, the single best thing you can do to your garden is to introduce water. Digging a small pond is relatively easy and one can be dug, lined, filled and planted in a weekend, or perhaps two. To be effective, ponds need not be deep, so vast earthworks are unnecessary and in fact can be counterproductive. Most small garden ponds will have a shelf at a depth of about eight inches (for marginal aquatic plants) and a central segment no deeper than two feet (for the likes of water lilies). But the pleasure this garden modification will bring is almost unbounded. As we all know, sitting and watching a pond, with the continual movement of light across its surface, is a pleasure in itself. Couple this of an evening with a drink and a comfy chair and the pleasure mounts.

The chief beneficiaries, though, are of course the insects and small mammals. By installing a pond you provide them with a watering hole. Bees will use lily pads like aircraft carriers, landing for a drink and then flying away. It is important during construction that you provide a beach area (in other words somewhere where there is a gentle slope into the pond) in order that non-flying small mammals (like hedgehogs) can not only get to the water to drink, but can get out of the water if they fall in.

I was looking over the pond here this summer and a streak of electric blue shot across the side of my vision. I remember catching glimpses of a kingfisher in just the same way while I walked around the lake as a teenager. The lake at home was large, several acres anyway. Like deep history, it seemed to hold secrets within its murky depths, until my father decided to have it netted. He made sure I was out of school for the weekend when it happened, knowing how excited I would be to finally come face-to-face with the monsters I had spent my childhood to that point stalking.

And then, suddenly, the mystery was broken. I was face-to-face with all the giant carp in the lake; some I had caught and recognised, others I didn't. I still remember a gargantuan mirror or ghost carp looking back at me sheepishly, as if it were embarrassed that the long myths of my childhood, the great and epic struggle to wrestle the 'big one' from the depths, now rested on its shoulders. It was big, certainly, but I had had similar-sized ones before. No pike was snared within the nets that day, but I knew they were there – I had seen them just under the surface. I guessed they would have pushed themselves into the soft sides of the lake as the nets passed. I had also seen dismembered carp floating upside down on the surface and small fish jumping in the late afternoon, confirming that there were pike there. So, the lake retained some of its mystery, but it transferred to the pike, the piranha of English fresh water. We never did pull one out, though.

Like the mirror carp, light reflects on water with unpredictable consequences. This ever-moving, ever-changing quality merged with constancy reflects something of the ancient but always fresh quality of truth. The long days (and nights) I spent by that lake, involved completely and utterly in my quest, consumed by it, are true. They are no less true today simply because they belonged to a different time and place. Neither is my father's smile as he revelled in my excitement – that smile, perhaps refracting his own childhood quest, consummated as it was with the largest ever perch caught in Essex – any less true today than it was then. These strands of meaning are my friends, not my enemy. They may be painful, painful in the extreme; but they are to me at least the waypoints of a grieving soul. What was can never not be simply because of the passage of time. The eternal remains, despite the endless and ongoing dance of light across water.

I am certain the kingfisher wouldn't visit our little pond in the home garden, which is perhaps fifteen feet across at its widest, if it weren't for the large, nineteen-acre reservoir at the bottom of the valley. The same goes for herons, which also occasionally visit our little wildlife pond. Though I have always found that I start to feel uncomfortable if I stare at a heron for too long.

I bought ducks before I bought a dog. Ducks are one of the few creatures that can walk, fly and swim. But because they are tri-capable (sea, air and land) they are also compromised (hopeless, really) in each domain. Just watching them waddle raises a smile. They make terrible mothers and their eggs, while good for baking, taste muddy and second rate in any other guise, at least to my palate. Besides, they lay them

189

anywhere, and in my experience usually on the edge of the pond. You are lucky if you can pick them before they knock them into the water.

Feeding the ducks has been a challenge. I started with normal grain feeders but the proximity of a ready supply of both food and water attracted the county's regiment of rats. After extensive enquiries, I discovered I could buy floating corn discs (together with specially modified duck food, which also floats) and while rats can swim, this has made them work much harder for their prize.

Runner ducks are my favourite of all. They stand as tall as a Labrador and walk with more grace than a normal duck. Nonetheless, ridiculous and elegant are two opposing adjectives that seem equally legitimate when applied to a runner. Seeing them wander around the garden in a pack was a joy but, unfortunately, I lost every last one to the fox.

Now I am left with my call ducks. Call ducks are small little things shaped like a regular duck. I was always told they were called 'call ducks' because they attracted wild ducks to the water through their calling. However, I have found the opposite to be true. We do get visiting wild ducks, though, no doubt refugees from the reservoir, at least one pair each spring. We get to watch them with their paddle of ducklings. Ducks will nest in the strangest of places; last year I saw a family emerge from a flower pot, and another at the side of a particularly dangerous road.

When we arrived we decided to throw a fence up around the pond, at least until our youngest child could swim. In among the chaos of the move and rush of unpacking, I made a textbook mistake – I forgot to put a gate in. This has meant that accessing the pond's margin requires climbing over the fence, which in turn has meant I rarely bother. Despite its proximity to the house I have labelled the whole place a wildlife garden and, other than occasionally hacking down a rose or hawthorn that has got too big, I have left it to get on with it. The result is an abundance of sedge, nettles, reeds, wild garlic and even some marsh marigold, which in the spring and early summer catches your eye every bit as violently as the dayglo yellow of a high visibility vest. The main beneficiaries of this horticultural sloth, however, are the insects, and to my greatest delight, the Odonata.

Odonata is not a name packed with romance, but refers to the insects more commonly called dragonflies and damselflies. They are every bit as rare and exotic to look at as their common names suggest. The habitat they like best of all is the water's edge. But it needs to be bright (not too shaded by trees, which is why I periodically hack them back) and rich with grasses. You can see the seasons through the pond just as adroitly as with any other part of the garden. Not long ago the pond was frozen over and I had to smash holes in the ice to make sure the ducks could drink; now, with the roses in full canter, it is a teeming mass of insect life. All of this helps as part of our organic programme. Water helps me to have a balanced population of insects and therefore to grow healthy plants without pesticides. Water is the single best thing you can give your garden; by favouring insects, it increases pollination and therefore the productivity of your vegetable patch while also feeding your avian choir to keep the sound of the garden sweet.

Chelsea Flower Show

After Sybilla's victory in Clacton, our discussions ranged on backwards and forwards about my work. After two growing seasons, Skymeadow was beginning to grow and fill markedly. I started to get compliments when people visited, and I even had a small gardening column in one of the local magazines. Despite all this, a final decision about my future employment hadn't been made, but now we had a driving licence in hand it had to be. Converting the small start I had made into the career I wanted seemed somewhat like an intractable problem; then two conversations changed everything.

The first was between Sybilla and me. We were having a late-night chat on the usual subject, over a glass of something, and she just looked at me and said, 'I've been thinking about it and you only live once; you should commit yourself completely to gardening. You don't want to have any regrets.'

That was it, the words just tumbled out. She had thought about it and given me her full support. She had released me. I had a pink ticket! For my part I agreed to support her desire to carry on with what I had nicknamed 'organic parenting', and not to berate her about not having help any more. Now she had a driving licence I couldn't assume I knew what was best for her, it was her call. In an exciting turnaround, the very day after we had this conversation, I got a breakthrough.

When we lived in London I had put some free time into working on the whole issue of modern slavery. Like many people, I thought slavery had ended centuries ago, but at a lecture in London the full and brutal truth, that modern slavery is alive and well, including in the city in which I lived, was brought home to me and I decided to try to do something about it. This led to a winding path and eventually I offered to help draft a document that helped to persuade an important think tank, called the Centre for Social Justice (CSJ), to make slavery the subject matter of its next big review. This was ideal because the CSJ was effectively the social conscience for the then Conservative government. The document worked. The report worked. Shortly thereafter, a new law gained Parliamentary assent: the 2015 Modern Slavery Act.

As a result of my small contribution to this effort, I got noticed by various other modern slavery campaigners as someone with a dog in the fight. One of these people, Mirabelle Galvin, had decided to do something really exceptional. Together with a number of friends she had decided to take a garden to the Chelsea Flower Show to raise awareness of modern slavery. She also knew I was a mad-keen gardener.

The very day after Sybilla and I had our late-night chat, Mirabelle got in touch.

'Charlie, we are taking a garden to Chelsea to raise awareness of modern slavery. Would you be our campaign director? You will get to understudy Juliet Sargeant, who has designed the garden, and you can run all aspects of the campaign. It won't be much, but we are happy to pay you too . . .'

I didn't have to think for long before giving my answer and what followed was a nine-month adventure filled with horticultural derring-do. The garden was a success and, in the end, it won a gold medal and also the People's Choice Award. We managed to help lots of new people take that first crucial step on the road towards doing something about modern slavery, which is merely recognising that it still actually happens. But for me other things also happened; I got to practise doing radio interviews, Juliet taught me how to behave in front of a camera (there are some basic ground rules, and it is amazing how much better you do if someone bothers to tell you what they are), and I got to meet a number of gardening editors. Some even started to ask me to write for them.

Finally, something that hinted towards a bona fide career started to peep through my gardening obsession. It was peeping through on the other side not just of the new garden I was building, but on the other side of my grief and on the other side of our move to the country and on the other side of my choices. The relief was searing.

In a horticultural sense, one of the most exciting things we did during the build-up to the Chelsea Flower Show was to name a rose. Letting a gardener loose in this way is a bit like giving a car nut half an hour in a Ferrari. The all new Modern Slavery Rose is a beautiful, almost apricot, floribunda and the lasting effect from Chelsea in the garden in Skymeadow is the clutch of them we now have growing in the rose garden.

Around this time we had another breakthrough; it came just in time for my work on the show garden. On the recommendation of a friend, a lady in her seventies arrived for an interview. The idea was she might do a couple of hours a week cleaning and babysit occasionally when we wanted to go out in the evenings with friends. Her name was Margaret. Sybilla and Margaret had a chat. They seemed to get on. I waited on tenterhooks.

Sybilla said that, after their chat, Margaret had asked her how my name was spelt, and then asked whether my father had been called David. It turned out that Margaret had helped my grandparents, including my grandfather whom I had never met. She knew my mother, my father and my uncle, and had quite strong opinions on all of them. She even remembered my elder brothers as children.

Margaret helps us clean the house, but that is not what she really does. She is an older person who has been there before, so Sybilla can occasionally run something by her, or get a bit of reassurance from her. Oddly, she has many of the same character traits that my mother had. That's what I had wanted for Sybilla, for both of us really. I think Margaret enjoys it too.

Coincidentally, Margaret and her son manage not one but three allotments and are, with the help of a couple of freezers, practically self-sufficient. She has been gardening, and talking to other gardeners, for a very long time. She often gives me sorely needed vegetable-growing instructions; but it is all the old country tips and sayings that I tell her she must write down. Margaret knew the name of the dog my father had as a young adult; in fact, she remembered the dog well, a lurcher called Dum Dum. Wow.

Exotic orchard

The land in the southwesterly corner of Skymeadow slopes back up towards the house like a French vineyard. Interestingly, a slope means that land with a southwest-facing aspect heats up significantly more quickly than if it were flat. I am gradually packing this slope with vines, figs and pomegranates. It is ambitious, from a horticultural perspective, but we get less rain and more sunshine hours here than in almost any other part of the country. The esteemed French champagne house Taittinger recently bought a vineyard in Kent; why shouldn't there be an exotic orchard in Essex?

Vines have been growing away happily in the UK for decades, particularly in the south-east. The technical advice is that anything south of a line from Pembroke to the Wash is pristine vine-growing territory. Actually, possibly due to climate change, much of the UK is becoming a suitable home for vines. This is not new, but the repetition of an ancient cycle.

My dad told me that the great oak trees in the abbey grounds in Bury St Edmunds were said to have rooted from the staves the monks used to grow vines in the Middle Ages. I have no idea if this is apocryphal – but it is certainly a charming thought. What is known for certain is that there was a medieval period of warming and the wine the monks of St Edmundsbury made was considered among the best in the world – and played no small part in building their power and wealth. I also know that English sparkling wines are now outcompeting champagnes in blind tastings.

For me, the most attractive of all conceivable foliage belongs to the fig. But the fig does so much more than merely provide us with one means of escape if we happen to lose all our clothes. It also produces what the Victorians would have called 'dainties'. The fruit of a fig is essentially a sweet and has all the flippancy, variety of texture and, if you are lucky, sweetness of any fruit truffle the chocolatiers of today can throw at you. The fig also has the advantage of not leaving you with that slightly sick feeling if, as I often do, you over-indulge. Nature at its most thoughtful!

There was a time when there were commercial fig orchards dotted around the south-east of England. Apparently, the last commercial fig orchard was at Clopton Hall in Suffolk. It shut its doors in the 1940s. Time spent reading about such things is very encouraging if you also happen to be spending time planting figs in your own garden.

Figs require slightly unusual treatment. Your objective with a fig is to restrict its root growth. If you do this you will get fruit; if you let the roots go the plant will produce foliage over fruit. This is why they often do well against a south-facing wall, planted hard in against the foundations.

Traditionally, people planted figs in fig pits. These are easy enough to make: you dig a hole and line it with four paving slabs (or three if its fourth is against a wall) and then crush twelve inches of hardcore into the bottom of the hole and plant the fig on top.

The soil in Skymeadow where I am planting figs is such thick clay that I wondered whether it might to a certain extent restrict root growth of its own accord. I also wondered whether this effect might be increased by using a circular planting hole. As it stands, I have planted many figs in Skymeadow, some in pits and others using different strategies such that the whole exotic orchard is to a certain extent an experiment, the results of which I will have in a few years' time. All this also means that figs do well in pots. When you tire of potting them into an ever-larger pot you can cut their roots back and return them to the same pot they were in but with new soil. I believe that at one of the Rothschild houses they have grown figs like this for the last hundred years with no ill effect.

The plant in the exotic orchard that causes me the greatest concern is the pomegranate. Like most other plantings here, I have had to extravagantly improve the drainage of my clay soil in order to even stand a chance. This is done with wide planting holes and buckets and buckets of horticultural grit. I also use the better pieces of flint that I find as I dig. For every foot of soil you dig here there is a good four inches of flint. In any case, my instinct tells me the pomegranate will not survive the cold if it also has wet feet. It is so often the combination of the two that leads to plant failure over winter.

By chance, during the conflict in Afghanistan my father-in-law got involved with a charity that was encouraging farmers there to replace their poppy crops with pomegranates (the area was famous for its pomegranates), and in so doing find a sustainable future that would keep them out of trouble. He made many hair-raising trips flying around in ancient Russian helicopters while my mother-in-law sat somewhat nervously in her kitchen in Gloucestershire. One thing he learnt and shared with me was that pomegranates will take much more easily if they are as large as possible when planted in their final destination.

This didn't stop Isaac and I excitedly picking apart a pomegranate that arrived in the weekly shop and planting twelve of the seeds. Of the twelve little saplings we have been growing, perhaps five or six will survive a few seasons in the conditions we can give them. These will have selected themselves for their eventual release into the wilds of north Essex.

Sybilla and I both have one grandparent of largely Jewish extraction. In both cases it was our father's father. So the exotic orchard is in some way a gentle nod to them, and to those forebears of ours who no doubt had to sharpen their wits and their hearts to survive the many European persecutions of Jews. But it is also a nod to the concept of 'father' generally; to the sense of protection that fatherhood brings, to the root that we are all grafted into in the general sense; and to my dad in particular. He was the sort of person who might have found my flowerbeds 'ordinary' but would have approved of the planting of an exotic orchard. The exotic orchard for us is about our own roots, but also the laying down of new ones, and the hope for harvest.

Vegetables

August is the month of harvest, and you'd better get on with it because, in my garden at least, all the rich variety to choose from narrows gradually until in September there are just marrows and pumpkins, and you have to start grocery shopping again.

I no longer grow vegetables simply because I think I should; vegetable growing here is now a matter of complete indulgence. This also means it takes place as close to the back door as possible.

The position of vegetable gardens has an interesting history. Originally, apart from in the very greatest houses, they were stationed where they could be easily tended and browsed by the family. This was expedient. When England's economy grew, at least around here largely because of the wool trade, and the great families had armies of retainers, vast walled gardens were constructed at a distance from the family home for the simple reason that other people tended them and could walk the produce up.

Now, many such houses are lived in by the descendants of the people who built them, but they no longer have armies of retainers. As a consequence their walled gardens are often derelict and can present a challenge to maintain. One solution that seems to be growing in popularity is to let them to a local flower grower. This is being driven by the increasing interest in organically grown British flowers. Where I grew up, I think my father considered the walled garden to be too good for vegetables and so it became a rose garden; the vegetables being cast out to a new arrangement ranged along its southern wall. Even so, vegetable growing was done on a prodigious scale and much of the meat and the vegetables we ate were grown at home.

Given that Skymeadow is tended by a vast army of one, my vegetables are as close as possible to the kitchen in which they will be eaten. I would recommend this general principle be considered by anyone laying out a new vegetable patch. However, it was not always thus. When we first arrived I was thinking in more extravagant terms. So, originally, the vegetable patch was in what is now the miniature arboretum. Then, having cottoned on properly to the labour dynamic, it moved up closer to the house, to a spare patch just below the berry orchard; but even there I found it was too distant to be easily browsable and, while sheltered, it lacked enough light for really triumphant vegetable growing.

So it moved again and now resides immediately outside my study at the bottom of the snaking sweet-pea border. Vegetables require a fair amount of tender loving care (and quite a lot of water) and I have found the browsability factor has markedly improved the quality of my produce; I can make innumerable little tweaks over the course of five-minute breaks taken throughout the day. I can't stress how much difference this has made; I need only open my study door and I am there in the middle of the vegetable garden.

As my vegetable growing has improved, the sense of indulgence – not misplaced indulgence but the legitimately and therefore energetically engaged variety – has increased considerably also. This carries with it a bounty that fills metaphysically not just physically. Making. Eating together. Cooking for others. Filling our hearts as we fill our bellies. All this I learnt at my father's stove. He was a great eater, and ate far more than I do, but I hold on to the dishes he so often cooked for me, just as closely as a baby does to its special rag.

I grow peas and carrots because freshly picked they taste sweeter than they ever do from the shops, and generally I try to grow things that are either genuinely better fresh or are hard to get in the shops. The sugars in many fruits and vegetables start to denature as soon as they have been taken off the plant. Lettuce I grow because Sybilla likes to have it in the garden, but in truth I find it a fiddle. Arctic King is a favourite, not so much for its hardiness but for the interesting velvety texture of its leaves. I like Tom Thumb for its ease of growing. The two vegetables that give me overwhelming amounts of pleasure, however, are from the same family: tomatoes and potatoes.

I always grow the single most unpopular tomato on the market, the one for which gardening snobs reserve their greatest vitriol: Moneymaker. It is the Lamborghini Countach of the tomato world, having been popular in the 1970s. The general problem with tomatoes is that the breeders have favoured blight immunity over flavour. The result is that many new varieties are healthy but have limited eating appeal. The horticultural world is stuck between the Scylla of a healthy tomato and the Charybdis of a flavoursome one. Moneymaker seems to work for me.

In addition to Moneymaker, I try a handful of other varieties each year. After the tomato beds have been planted, I always have some left over, which invariably get stuffed into grow bags or given away. Like squashes, I have grown left-overs very successfully in half-matured heaps of compost. I sow my tomatoes early, always before February is out, because they require a long growing season. They sit in the porch and half get planted out under cloches in April, with the others going out after the last frost. I leave no hostages to fortune because there is nothing that sums up high summer more perfectly to me than a handful of warm tomatoes straight off the vine, particularly if they are co-opted for breakfast.

Much of my vegetable growing is organised around a loose concept of breakfast. During the week, I all too often fail to eat breakfast; with all the other jobs that need doing outside there is no time before the school run and I have lost interest in it afterwards. However, this should not be thought to mean I don't love breakfast and my weekend breakfasts are among my greatest eating pleasures. A perfectly poised and delivered breakfast, eaten at the cusp of the point at which the day can be said to have truly started, when the house is still quiet, is the best of all meals. For me, the thing that would most likely kill the pleasure of breakfast is to eat one that is too large and then sinks the rest of the morning. My rule is anything that can be carried on a single slice of toast is not too large. But an awful lot can be carried on a single slice of toast.

The subject matter of what goes on the toast changes with the seasons, of course. Spring often brings a bed of spinach (and some roughly chopped garlic) fried in a nob of butter, seasoned heavily and flavoured with a pinch of nutmeg and a pinch of turmeric. A freshly laid egg fried and placed gingerly on top. The butter stained yellow with spice, soaks down through the spinach and creates rivulets on the buttered toast. Delicious. Summer might see a slathering of butter and gage jam, a fried Portobello mushroom and a dressing of bacon lardons fried in olive oil with garlic. And so the happy weekend dance goes on. In the autumn, before a day of digging, I must try to remember to eat breakfast during the week even if I don't feel like it; otherwise by about twelve my body tends to hit a sugar-deprivation wall. This is remedied, as I imagine it is by gardeners up and down the country, with a long drink of Ribena and a couple of packs of Hula Hoops. Now I should stop.

I feel there are two approaches to potatoes. The first is to grow them on scale with the intention of providing a main food source for your family from June into winter. This is easy to do and (subject to the attention of slugs) potatoes store well if you simply leave them in the ground. However, this approach requires giving them a lot of space. The second is to grow small batches of the potatoes that you really enjoy eating and that the shops don't always have. These become a treat for your family when they mature and for as long as stocks last. Like wine, potatoes vary hugely in flavour, but they also vary in texture and for me this is the most important distinction.

I don't like potatoes that make good mashers (think white and fluffy in texture). Instead, I like potatoes with a waxy, almost crisp texture and a nutty taste (in much the same way as I like a waxy white wine). Pink Fir Apple is a main crop potato with just these qualities, and Anya, its genetic offspring, is good for an early crop. I give them what space I have available.

Last year, I grew a potato called Kestrel. It is very reliable and ideal if you want a white fluffy masher (which I didn't particularly). Everyone in our family seems to get several nicknames and one usually predominates. Our youngest daughter Celestia generally gets called Kestrel, so in a weak moment I picked up a sack of Kestrel potatoes. I thought it might get Sybilla more interested in the veg patch. However, following last year's success, I am greatly upscaling our tomato and pea crops this year so there is no room for such whimsical purchases. It is worth remembering that if you are really pushed for space all potatoes will grow perfectly happily in a sack or even an old dustbin, so long as you provide drainage holes.

I also love to grow cucurbits. These are a confusing bunch variously described as squashes, marrows, pumpkins, courgettes and gourds, but they are all cucurbits. If you wish to make sense of these high-performance vegetables the central thing to grasp is that the true distinction is between summer squashes (which tend to grow on bushes, like patty pan) and winter squashes (which tend to grow on vines, like Turk's turban or the classic jack o'lantern). Summer squashes are harvested in summer as they ripen (and generally the skin can be eaten); winter squashes are harvested in the autumn (and the skin is hard to the point of being difficult to cut). The courgette, if left, will become a squash. None of mine ever are; courgette and chilli pasta is a very popular dish in this house.

I have found that some years favour cucurbits and others don't. I am not sure what the determining factor is in this, but given they need a long growing season, I wonder whether it might hinge on the general level of light and the number of sunshine hours afforded to us in any given year. I grow squashes to eat and I have sometimes made an old Suffolk favourite, marrow and ginger jam, with end-of-season leftovers. It is a great cold buster during winter. In the autumn and winter, we also add the flesh to stews. In the summer, I love to take a patty pan (which looks like a flying saucer and is ready when it's the size of your hand) and scoop out the seeds. I then stuff it with salt, pepper, smoked paprika and blue cheese and bake it for half an hour or so. The easiest dinner you could wish for. Some squashes have a nice nutty flavour, others are a little bland. Bland ones can be immeasurably lifted by sprinkling them liberally with smoked paprika before baking.

However, even if a cucurbit never made it into our kitchen I would still grow them for their extravagance in the border. To my mind, Turk's turban looks excellent in or near a border. It will sprawl in a vine-like way but the fruits are so marvellous to behold it can create great late season interest. Quite a lot of my vegetable growing does take place in the border. I plant lots of artichokes in my borders, and they work very well in the rose garden, so long as they are given enough room. I frequently let them flower because they make such a dramatic contribution. Rhubarb is another vegetable that can help out in a tricky, slightly shady corner within a flower border. I grow vines as standard in flowerbeds too.

Vegetables and fruit are a matter of complete indulgence in this household; it is a form of indulgence that we have all been able to reach out to and touch, even when, especially when, our collective desire to push back a sense of loss has been strongest.

Autumn

Eagle

The little fledgling eagle from my box grew and grew over the summer; I shared our successes with it; I shared our garden with it. It had become as sharp as a spear, with clear yellow eyes, yellow like the sun they reflected. My grief grew through its feathers, all the little shards of myself I had lost to the business of life; the shards of others, lost also. The eagle taught me that grief is nothing to be afraid of. It is simply one corollary of love, and love is good. Besides, the eagle seemed to bring with it extreme precision: precision of feeling, of thought and of heart. Precision I had always wanted, but never been capable of. I loved the eagle. I had learnt my grief was a gift, but the eagle led me to other gifts too. The eagle taught me more about the harrow.

To start with, the eagle wouldn't leave my shoulder; always a wildling, but always there. For my part I was fascinated with it. Its truthful elegance, its aching beauty. One September, as the soft golden light of autumn slanted past us, it took to the sky and flew. I could see my grief soaring high above me, with power, intent and purpose. I turned and walked back up the hill to the house. The eagle settled again, as light as a feather. Loyal too; it had my back.

I have a strong recollection of a September evening during my childhood. I might have been sixteen and I was away at school. I noticed for the first time the slanting softening autumnal light, golden as if it had fallen directly from the throne of heaven, from the family of peace. This quality gave me a sense of indescribable peace; a joyfully drenched silken reflectiveness. It was the joy of losing oneself and finding oneself, as if the play on the two were guaranteed at a point somewhere beyond time. It was a moment before the eagle that nonetheless pointed to it.

I had needed the courage to open my box. I knew that. I had needed the courage to look the eagle in the eye. I knew that too. Meeting my grief honestly had caused it to transform into this powerful creature, but the eagle's principal lesson was to look with unblinking eyes. Eagles don't flinch. Flinching has no purpose in nature, flinching spells disaster. The eagle was teaching me about the harrow.

We may be small but no one can steal from us the power we have to look honestly. In the moment my father spelt out on a board his own experience with anxiety, I knew progress was possible. That moment felt like a magnificent discovery. But it was only to be the first rung on the ladder. The discovery happened because my father reached past my flinching as he slowly and with frustration used all he had left, his eyes, to look first at a colour and then at a letter on a plastic board held by a nurse in order to spell out his truth for me. I got the map from him late, I got it literally just in time, but I got it

212

exactly when I needed it and I struck out straight away. I discovered that he knew what I knew. I felt there were longer arms beneath me, beneath us both.

I quizzed my mother. They had been inseparable at his moment of greatest struggle with the harrow; a moment long before me. She poured further soothing balm on me and told me all about it. She had known; I hadn't. They didn't want to manufacture anything. Why would you? And yet my father knew me, and he had left clues for me. But at the time I flinched too much to get close to them. He had told me once how, on a bright summer's day, while in the clouds above his home, he had imagined flying his Zlín into his bedroom window; how the imagined act held an absurd attraction. There was a clue too in the fact that our laughter always turned fastest on points of existential absurdity; on the material that sat just beyond the range.

The eagle has since helped me see all this; to see the resounding sense in it. I think those of us who live with a harrow need this. It's not madness – it's a type of perspective that keeps us sane. It's a fact of existence for those whose anxiety forces them to look through and around danger. Perspective is the gift; the biochemical cost can be borne if you learn not to flinch. That is what the eagle in the box taught me, that is what grief taught me. I tasted it first as a sixteen-year-old on a September evening when my soul fell to the outstanding beauty of soft golden light. I quest for it now every day of the year.

Were there those in the human family whose purpose was to sit always somewhere on the edge, always watching with the eyes of an eagle? Ready to signal, ready to raise up a greater chance of survival while others ate and slept? I had seen in the eagle not logic but purer, higher reason. Was the eagle telling me I had to make friends with my anxiety? Telling me it was a gift, an old friend?

213

Today I not only, at the very first hint, throw open the door to anxiety but actively welcome it across the threshold like a friend. This is where the journey back from the edge started for me. The chains on a harrow are only tight as you rush away from them. If you rush towards it there is no tension; there can't be. I started this journey after I made the discovery that I was not alone with my harrow, that my father had been harrowing too, but it took the eagle to round off the lesson into something not just useable, but deeply comfortable. Eagles look honestly and without flinching.

Now that we have set up a home in the countryside, my early struggles with anxiety, particularly the searing anxiety of my youth, feel pleasingly far off. I am still more anxious than most, but the frozen metallic stall is very infrequent and very infrequently visible. I am an old hand now. I practise looking without flinching, just as the eagle does. Sybilla has learnt to know when things are challenging. It would be easier for her if it was other, but there it is.

The older we both get, the more we are minded not to worry so much about the vicissitudes of human nature, the challenges of flesh and blood. A gift of age, a gift of the hard edges, pushed into so frequently that they are no longer hard. We used to be more squeamish, not in the sense that we would flinch at others, but in the sense that we would flinch at ourselves; for our foolishness, for our fear, for our immaturity. Over time we have learnt that the guns we turn on ourselves are usually the ones that spill the most blood. They make us run from the harrow and as we do the chains always fasten grimly around us. British military doctrine has long held that the only answer to an ambush is to run directly at it; this is the only act your ambushers won't expect. If you run away, you are toast. This is what the eagle taught me about the harrow: only as you rush at it do the chains loosen.

Winter's approach

My principal coping mechanism for life generally is, of course, to live in the countryside. Living in the countryside exposes you to softer and altogether more pleasant anxieties of another kind, those that are tied to the seasons; these I have learnt to welcome also. There is a clear 'cash back' moment for us each summer as the children run in the meadow, their invariably un-brushed hair caught and turned golden by the declining evening light, but winter pushes us all back into the house and therefore the geography of our family life shrinks gradually until it reaches what feels like a very thin point. In short, winter forces us to exchange a seven-acre home for one with four walls. The children grumble about going outside in the gloaming and I have to devise increasingly flamboyant strategies to get them out. Last year, building a willow igloo caught Beatrice's imagination and we built it each night after school using light from an iPhone torch.

Sybilla and I consider ourselves relatively hardy country folk, but winter in a place as set apart as this has a way of catching and magnifying any sense of isolation you may already feel. So for us the approach of winter still carries with it some trepidation. In truth, from July I am dimly aware of momentary flutters. That is all they are. Fleeting and infrequent moments as I go about my daily chores where the pre-emotion of panic emerges for a second and hovers, saying something about the fact that summer doesn't last for ever. A gnawing concern about something vague and uncertain but irreducibly tied to the fact of another winter. Sometimes, for only a moment, I feel like the best man who can't enjoy dinner because he knows his speech is on the other side of it.

These pangs have more or less gone by the time of the vernal equinox, and then I am excited for winter. Perhaps they are a prompt to check the barns are full. An inherited echo; the vestiges of a seasonal alarm clock, selectively bred into my ancestors who for thousands of years depended on their agrarian livelihoods. Either way, as Christmas nears the pangs are long gone, because by Christmas I am committed to the season. After all, there would be no benefit to a prompting at Christmas – there is nothing left to gather, and nature is nothing if not efficient.

Winter sits at the opposite end of the year to harvest, and there is no getting around that fact. Winter is the beginning as harvest is the conclusion. Before the introduction of inexpensive air travel this was an unassailable fact of existence. As with everyone above a certain age, I have shaken the hand of someone whose grandparents knew real winter hunger. Like a ghoulish waltzing pair, winter and hunger were a consistent presence in the life of country folk until the mass

216

production of corn enabled the Victorians to feed children white bread. This brought the horrible waltz to an end, but stored up trouble of another kind for their grandchildren. Despite being well fed, winter hunger still sits in the hearts of the lonely and dispossessed, even in high summer. But the destination must always be harvest.

Main avenue

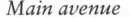

Main avenue is rather a grand name for something that started life in our first year as a grass strip (roughly three sweeps with the mower, about twelve-foot wide) mown through the meadow, simply to extend the path that runs past the house and through the garden. We had to move a five-bar gate to make the paths progress into the meadow uninterrupted – this incredibly simple act delivered a huge amount of visual pleasure. But for ages that was the totality of main avenue: an open gate and a nine-foot mown track.

Nonetheless, avenues (even ones made of no more than tall grass for four months of the year) are somehow intrinsically stately. They march from one place to another. Not only do they bring order, rhythm and flow to a landscape, they also speak triumphantly of progress, of new beginnings, of confirmation. That is what they physically do as you move along

219

them to a conclusion. They are inherent celebrations. They do to a landscape what Handel's 'Zadok the Priest' did for the coronation.

In our third year, main avenue finally got its trees, and it was a transformational moment for Skymeadow. Almost the only thing (apart from our friends) that I miss from our time living in London is the ability to celebrate life's triumphs (or commiserate its occasional troughs) by having delicious food delivered to your door. Hassle-free calories are one of life's supreme luxuries. I remember with crystal clarity one evening eating sushi. Sybilla wasn't drinking so I was casting around for something that didn't require opening a bottle of wine. I had some posh whisky stashed in a cupboard from Christmas and I thought, *Why not?* It was a legendary pairing that left an explosion of flavour and fullness in my mouth; a sort of ecstatic brimming over.

I know now this pairing is one way of achieving what the Japanese call umami, the fabled fifth taste that complements sweet, sour, bitter and salty. Umami is linked to the other four tastes in the sense that it somehow mysteriously completes them – and yet it is standalone in the sense that it can be absent. This is what structure gives to a garden: visual umami. I have discovered that so many of my highest points in the garden have a sort of visual umami to them. They are the moments when the eye experiences an ecstatic brimming over and the heart soars. This happens when the picture is made mysteriously so much more than the sum of its constituent parts – precisely what planting main avenue did to Skymeadow.

In the end I decided to plant main avenue with the small cherry tree *Prunus incisa*, 'The Bride'. For a short period in spring the Bride produces ice-white flowers. It has a brief flowering period but is all the more beautiful for that. It must

220

be savoured. Like many cherries, the bark of the tree has little grey eyes in circles around its circumference, which it uses to photosynthesise when it has no leaves. The leaves adopt a rich crimson colour in the autumn before they fall. Although not as iridescent, the colour is something approaching the unexpected splendour one gets from that most fine autumnal performer, the blueberry bush. Finally, the delicate and beautiful little Bride catches something of the softness of the Essex landscape. Attempting to catch and magnifying this essential quality has been my constant task in the garden here.

As I planted the last cherry tree, I stood up to look back along the double row and experienced an overwhelming sense of visual umami. The avenue had added so much more than even I expected was possible. It is powerful stuff, this umami, and I rushed off to do the school run grinning, and was still smiling somewhat inanely as I went to bed that night.

I remember the sensation of umami in the garden in much the same way as I remember its culinary counterpart. I can hold in my mind's eye exactly how I felt after I had seen the cherry trees in place, just as I can the first time I accidentally mixed whisky and sushi. Capability Brown famously described how a turn in a river might act as a comma or a thicket of trees a full stop. His landscapes deliver an overwhelming concentration of optical flavour and fullness. But equally there is something of this same visual taste in a freshly edged flowerbed or that moment when the coming together of two plants suddenly makes a picture. In any case, the quest to create visual umami, and of the highest possible intensity, is one of the things that keeps me heading out into the garden.

Of course, an avenue is merely a piece of grammar in the general business of garden design. While the word 'avenue' conjures images of stately homes and lime trees marching off into the middle distance, in fact you don't need a stately pile

221

or anything like it to benefit from an avenue. Six pieces of box topiary, paired with each other in either matching or asymmetrical shapes, will deliver to the urban garden the same effect grammatically as a lime avenue delivers to a great park. They both provide a beginning, a middle and an end. They both separate one area from another while also providing the means of travel between them. They both lead to a conclusion and carry an air of triumph and mastery.

Three is an endlessly interesting number to the human mind and, I think, is the minimum number of pairs necessary to create this effect. Two always looks wrong and a single pair is not an avenue but a perfectly legitimate arch. Of course, these rules really relate to the number of shapes. For example, eight willows woven together might make a single arch, but never doubt the fact that there is real poetry in numbers. At its most basic level this accounts for the common advice to only ever plant in ones, threes, fives, sevens, nines and so on. Numbers of shapes are a critical factor in the overall level of optical virtue created.

The first thing you need to consider when planting an avenue is what you want its ultimate height to be. I chose the Bride, a small tree usually marketed as suitable for small gardens, precisely because I don't want their eventual height to overwhelm Skymeadow or break the sense of it being a single garden moated by sky. An avenue of thumping great limes would have, eventually, cut Skymeadow in half, like a giant cleaver.

The second key question when creating an avenue is to consider its width. Avenues can legitimately be either wide or narrow. This is, after all, a matter of taste. I am a romantic, and I view the making of a garden as the effort to tame a wild space and make it comfortable for humans. When I planted our avenue, I chose a width that means the widest branches of the trees I used might one day reach towards each other, Sistine Chapel like. With taller trees you can hope that the higher branches might mingle above the heads of those who walk the avenue. While this is all subjective, my general rule is that the narrower the avenue, the more intimate, and to my way of thinking, the better. One of Rosemary Verey's seminal compositions was her laburnum avenue under-planted with alliums. It covers a surprisingly small footprint and would be easily replicable in many urban gardens – a more intimate or rewarding avenue is hard to imagine.

A final variation on this theme that is worth mentioning is the use of a tunnel. A tunnel is just a super-intimate avenue. In the gardens at Highgrove there is a pear tunnel. Bringing fruiting, delicious bounty into this already intensely intimate and romantic space creates, for me at least, a fever pitch of horticultural excitement. For anyone with the budget to create the metalwork (wood would rot as you waited for the pear trees to grow), I would highly recommend a pear tunnel. I would like one.

Main avenue was finally in, but Skymeadow's structure would not be complete until the six hundred and fifty feet of hawthorn hedge that was intended to support the avenue, enclose the rest of the exotic orchard and shield Isaac's football pitch was also in. I felt somewhat weary thinking about this, but I knew it had to be done.

Autumn colours

I struggled through the job of raking up leaves by hand this year. When they were all neatly stacked behind the log cabin, ready to make leafmould, and my arms ached like anything, I thought, *You silly ass, why didn't you just connect the bagging system to the mower and pick them up mechanically?* Generally I am not the type to worry too much about fallen leaves looking untidy, but this year I was gathering them all up to make as much leafmould as possible in order to leaven my heavy clay soil.

While compost is made by the action of bacteria rotting down organic matter, leafmould is made by the action of fungus. For it to work, the leaves need to be gathered together (for example, in a wire cage) and they need to stay damp. If you have ever picked up a handful of soil on the floor of an ancient woodland you will see it is black and crumbly, and this is what you are trying to make. The challenge for me is that I have a lot of chestnut leaves and they take much longer to break down than, for example, ash or oak leaves. I have separated them out (broadly speaking) and my chestnut-leaf pile may take several years before it is ready. If I was a betting man, I would bet it will all get pressed into service within the compost heap while still in a half-cooked state.

During the autumn there is a moment before leaf fall when the trees scream at us and demand to be looked at; it is their time. This is the moment to visit the nearest arboretum. Last autumn, a great beech tree at Westonbirt, its leaves burnished orange, burnt itself into my visual memory. The colours of fire lick through our hedges and woodlands; gold, orange, brown and red. The fire is all-consuming and soon we will have the ember of it only in our hearts.

The whole question of colours, and how to use them, is of course at the heart of any garden and it is in the autumn when I carefully think through the various choices I have made that year and how well they have worked. There is much technical discussion as to what colours go with what other colours, and even whole books on the subject. In truth, I disregard most of this advice and just go with what I like. People can be a bit precious, and most plants can be easily moved. Sometimes clashes of colour amuse me or startle me, and so they remain. I planted a peach-coloured rose (which in retrospect was a bit of a dodgy purchase) next to a scarlet rose campion and the clash made me feel physically sick, but that is as bad as it has ever got.

On the other hand, certain combinations go together so well there is no denying it. One such combination is black and gold (or yellow, as you will). Our barn needed flowerbeds along one side and I dug them in our first year. The barn's weatherboarding is black, so I chose yellow flowers for the bed. Yellow daffodils, yellow wallflowers, lady's mantle, yellow salvias and five Arthur Bell roses. Together they keep the yellow-gold theme going throughout the better part of the year, and each season it has got better and better. It just works.

In this household, the transition to autumn, and a celebration of the season's colours, is marked in the sky too. I love fireworks and let them off with the slightest excuse. Children's and pets' birthdays (most of which are in the autumn) are marked with fireworks, as is the arrival of friends and frankly anything else I can think of so long as the firework cupboard isn't bare. Like roses, a handful of rockets is enough to immeasurably lift the mood of a winter evening and bring smiles to the faces of whoever happens to be in the Hart household at the time. Add a tipple of glühwein and a mince pie, and winter starts to sparkle.

Gardening and letting off fireworks are in some ways remarkably similar activities. In both cases, your object is to surprise and delight. Both activities, if they are to be done well, require pre-planning and foresight, and you want a combination of colours and visual shapes. Clearly with fireworks this process is sped up. In fact, blink and you miss it. But the fleeting and ephemeral aspect heightens the sense of excitement. Both activities are expensive and carry a small modicum of risk.

I like to think both activities are also in some sense audacious; one in the horizontal (largely) and the other in the vertical (hopefully). Creating great booms of colour on land or in the sky is about fighting back; taking new ground; refusing to stand on either grief or death; trusting in progress; and all the prizes that come from never giving up. This is about life, and life lived abundantly. This is place where it matters. This is a quest for triumph; a triumph whose colour wheel licks through our hedges every autumn.

The central difference is that for fireworks the sky is your flowerbed – and Skymeadow provides the best possible raw material. With every flash and boom the whole valley lights up and is lent, for a split second, a colourful and thunderous frame. Imagine my delight when I discovered that the Japanese word for a firework, *hanabi*, can be translated literally as 'fiery flower'. I can extend the reach and scope of Skymeadow immeasurably, and, if only for a few minutes at a time, garden in the sky. This opportunity comes just as the real garden descends under a blanket of leaves. It is something I look forward to every year; a consolation prize as the evenings draw in.

Sharing the garden

A number of obvious challenges emerge from the fact that I share this garden with my family. Many are just what you might imagine and include, *inter alia*, children swinging on the delicate lower branches of magnolia trees; building camps and not tidying them away; picking (or rather tearing) numerous flowers from their stems the day before we open the garden; compacting the soil in the vegetable beds while eating everything before I get a look in; hiding cuddly toys in the long grass so that when I go over them with the mower there is an explosion of stuffing, which is impossible properly to clear up and my personal *bête noire*; and kicking gravel into the lawn with the result that it dims the blades on the push mower and can do much worse if it comes zinging out, colliding, for example, with my shin. But these are all challenges that reside at the tactical level and can be addressed with a little gentle persuasion and/or blackmail.

There are also, however, challenges at the strategic and structural level. For example, autumn is all about football, certainly in this household. I know almost nothing about the game, but Isaac is teaching me about it in my mid-thirties. It is one of his great loves. Isaac's football pitch is responsible for one tranche of the six hundred and fifty feet of new hedge that still needed to go into Skymeadow. His football pitch hasn't quite been a thorn in my side. In fact, I am grateful and pleased we live in a place that has enough space for him to have a football pitch, even if it is half-sized; it is the pay-off he enjoys for having a garden-crazed father. But, on the other hand, even a half-sized football pitch needs careful thinking through if it also happens to be slap-bang in the middle of an intensively thought-through garden. It presents some challenges.

The most obvious challenge was the garish white plastic football goals. First, one goal arrived. You can't have a proper football pitch without a goal. The old habit of simply tossing a jersey on the ground for each post apparently isn't sufficient these days, and, I accepted, netting is useful to catch the ball (and prevent it flying through into neighbouring parts of the garden). Then Isaac wanted to hold a football-themed birthday party and this was to include an elaborate tournament of five-a-side games over the course of an afternoon. Accordingly, a second goal appeared because, clearly, a football pitch with a single goal was silly. So much was clear. All the time, Isaac was skilfully working his grandmother, the purveyor of garish plastic football goals.

The party, needless to say, passed off well. However, I was left with two thumping great eyesores obscuring the view down into the valley, to the left of main avenue. I needed a solution and moving them up to the barn and back every time he wanted to kick a ball around was not practical (for him, or me). So I began to think of the football pitch as its own garden room, like all the others, fashioned by its relation to main avenue. I jiggled it around a bit, but there was no way to use the contours of the land to obscure the posts, without it being at such a great distance from the house it would never be used. I decided the only solution, ultimately, was to plant it out using a hedge. With this in mind, I found a natural place to the left of main avenue where the new hedge, in addition to obscuring the pitch, would provide greater definition and, importantly, additional shelter to the exotic orchard, further protecting it from northerly winds.

But, as we all know, hedges not only take time to plant (they have to be entered into the already-packed garden schedule of new jobs), they also take years to grow. In the meantime, I simply couldn't stand the way in which the bright plastic goal posts drew my eye every time I looked out into the valley. My solution was to paint them. Isaac now has green-coloured goals. This will do while we all wait for a hedge to grow.

But the football pitch isn't the end of the matter, merely a selective example. Collectively, the children want camps, trampolines, swings, climbing frames, sandpits and garish tricycles (and then eventually bicycles), and all these items need to be sited or stored somewhere. But I wouldn't have it any other way and as we all sit together on the grass in the middle of the rose garden in high summer and dither and talk and dither some more; the garden feels alive precisely because of the troop of humans who are fortunate enough to call it home.

This sense of home extends to our beasts and fowl, too. For me, a garden that isn't shared with the full panoply of

231

creatures that man has had the foresight to domesticate wouldn't feel like a garden attached to a home at all. It would resemble a museum piece held in aspic. Domestication took place because an area of mutual benefit, a value in the partnership, was identified. As with children, each type of animal will take with one hand and give with another; but the garden taken as a whole will thrive as it is shared. If the gift of warm tomatoes marks out high summer, the rest of the summer, and the rest of the year (save a short interval in late winter), is marked out by a small warm gift of another kind: eggs. Reaching into the laying box for a handful of warm fresh eggs is a reminder of harvest even in the months when the garden itself sleeps. It is possible to sit and watch chickens for hours and remain completely content; like a fire, or the waves on the sea, they embody perpetual motion.

While we were away on holiday an old friend came to housesit. The friend in question is a brilliant academic and writer but animal husbandry is a new skill for him. I, perhaps unfairly, left him with all manner of creatures to tend. Disaster struck. I got a sad message from him. For two mornings, he had gone out to feed the chickens only to find several birds inexplicably dead. Worse, he wasn't able to reach me to ask what to do. He thought they might be allergic to him, or shocked by a new person bringing them food each morning.

They were neither allergic to him (nor did they have bird flu, a reportable disease) but had been hounded by an infestation of red mite, very common in the middle of summer. It must have got out of control while I had been away. This horrible little mite was sucking the life from them. The mites hide in nooks and crannies during the day and emerge at night to feed.

A tell-tale sign of an emerging issue is when hens, quite sensibly, refuse to return to the coop to roost at night.

However, usually the first sign of mite is when I walk away from the coop itching. The mite will bite humans but thankfully they don't take up permanent residence on us. It is easy to fix, particularly if, like me, you have a plastic coop that can be easily disassembled and scrubbed down. Once cleaned, you have to spread diatomaceous earth around the chickens and the coop itself. Another trick, if your coop allows it, is to open it to the sunlight during the day. When it comes to mites, sunlight really is the best antiseptic. I feed my hens garlic too, which in any case they enjoy eating and which may help to deter infestations. The first frosts put an end to mites, as they do to much of the rest of the garden.

I love chickens, and I am grateful for their daily gift to us. I thought that explaining these losses to the children was going to be tricky. The children had, after all, named each chicken and more than half the flock came from eggs we incubated in the house. They had literally lived in our home with us for their first few months. In fact, the children took the news more or less in the same way that they would if we had said, 'Sorry, no pizza this evening, you will have to have pasta.' Even so, it was a sad business, but unfortunately, as all gardeners know, the other side of harvest is the worry about its loss.

The major loss to our harvest last year was to mice. First, I noticed the sweet peas were being got at in the coldframe. Then I noticed the table peas I am growing this year were being got at in the coldframe too. Then I noticed that the peas I had planted out were destroyed. The only peas that survived were an insurance batch in an old wheelbarrow because the mice couldn't scale its sides.

The only solution that doesn't involve a long and agonising death (as poison melts their innards) is cats. But this sort of decision would have to get past headquarters. After a certain amount of lobbying, headquarters agreed. Isaac found a single kitten on Gumtree that looked adorable. Because he had taken it upon himself to search, and he had come up trumps, I felt obliged to follow through with his selection. Then everything moved very quickly. I drove to somewhere near Romford to pick up the kitten. When I arrived at the house, I noticed the kitten had a brother. I felt bad about separating them and after a quick phone call I returned with two kittens, one each for Beatrice and Florence.

In fact, their ownership, as with all our pets, is more complicated than that. What generally happens is that one child gets principal ownership (50 per cent) with the remainder distributed among the others, usually, though not always, in equal shares. This means everyone has a pet they own, but ownership also, to some degree or other, of every other pet. The ownership of all our dogs, cats, chickens and ducks is carefully carved up and held in trust in this manner. Two new friends joined our merry troop (Collie and Pipkin) and, needless to say, everyone was in kitten heaven for several weeks while I was back on my hands and knees scrubbing poo off the carpet.

I always push for extra animals, while Sybilla's is the voice of reason. Usually this means we do a deal in which I promise to remove any accidents from the carpet and take the lead when it comes to food and vet visits. Given the age of our children, this is a fair trade and Sybilla holds me, albeit gently, to the terms of trade. Interestingly, for someone who is, by nature, about as gentle as they come, Sybilla, in direct contrast to most other people, finds pets more appealing the older they get. An old sea dog will receive far more attention from her than a newly born, conventionally 'cute' puppy.

Getting the cats was great, but for Sybilla and I nothing could rival the sheer excitement of getting our first dog together. Seymour is a chocolate Labrador and he has stolen each of our hearts. Just like on the night before we moved to Peverels, on the night before I went to pick up Seymour I barely slept a wink. The naming process had started in earnest before Isaac and I made the drive up to Timworth, just outside Bury St Edmunds, to pick him up, but nothing was confirmed until we met him. When we first saw Seymour he looked like a little cocktail sausage.

Names in the running included Biscuit, Patch and Pebble, but in the end Sybilla said Seymour with a sort of authority that stuck. Sybilla had always wanted to call a dog Seymour and it had almost happened ten years previously when her mother's shy golden Lab was ravaged behind a dry stone wall in Gloucestershire by her neighbour's collie. When informed of the collie's behaviour the neighbour said, with a look of sheer outrage, 'He wouldn't do a thing like that!' Well, he had. The resultant litter was small and my mother-in-law was left with one puppy that we looked at with longing eyes. But we were living in London and Isaac had just been born. We weren't ready for a puppy so we shied away, sad and disappointed, but in agreement that it was the right decision. Like getting married or buying a house, getting a dog shouldn't be entered into lightly. It ended well because the puppy in question is now a grand old lady called Ping and she comes to stay at Peverels along with my in-laws from time to time.

I asked Isaac if he wanted to give Seymour a middle name. Quick as a flash he said 'Mercy'. I am not sure why (and if you asked Isaac now he probably wouldn't have a clear idea either), but it has been a very appropriate name, because through the rough patches Seymour has been something of a strength and stay for both Sybilla and me. Dogs do this. Seymour is my stalwart gardening companion, and has kept me company through it all. He stood guard as I dug the rose garden (only occasionally peeling off to hunt mice in a favourite corner of Skymeadow). He was there as I planted main avenue. He has watched on as I have both killed and coddled plants. Many times, when it has been just us, he has looked at me sideways and I have looked back through tears; he always comes closer, never shies away. I love him.

I strongly believe dogs are good for children, and they are good for adults for that matter too. They are good for our health, our heart and our soul. In unguarded moments, you can catch Sybilla singing to Seymour, in much the same way as she did to each of the children when they were babies. I think dogs level the mood in a home, calming the highs and taking the edge off the lows. Seymour is technically 50 per cent Isaac's dog, with the remainder split equally between his three sisters, but it is Celestia who has grown up with him from the word go. Many times I have come back into the house to see Seymour and Celestia sleeping peacefully together in his basket. Her head rests on his belly, protected on either side by his hind- and forelegs.

Seymour is not tall, and while he has a golden temperament, he is not the cleverest of fellows. On the other hand, he is handsome and easily the poshest person I know. His Kennel Club name is Miracle Man, and he is descended from a long line of Labradors, with incredibly romantic names such as Harbour Master, Sandylands, Moonlit Harbour, Tranquil Sea and Fireflintof. One of his sixteen great-great-grandparents was called Hazelbeach Hoorah Henry of Llanstinan. I suspect he was a jolly fellow. And from there, I can see him descended from the grand old Labradors of Labrador, seafaring princes one and all.

Seymour has one Achilles heel. He has a gargantuan food obsession that Sybilla says is akin to living with someone struggling with a sex addiction. From chicken scraps to the bodily excretions of children via plastic toys, there appears to be nowhere his gut hasn't, at one stage or another, taken him. Certainly he is the only dog I know who will scavenge directly from the veg patch or take fruit off trees in the orchard. He is welcome to both for he has brought a true harvest of love into our home.

My hearth

In our family, we light fires as soon as there is the faintest chill in the air and keep them going until the evenings become bearable, usually in late spring. There is no rule against having a fire in the summer, and I enjoy one if it is damp and there is an evening chill. In midwinter, every morning I feed the animals and then light a fire before taking a quick turn outside, sometimes with a torch, sometimes without. In a far corner of the garden I often smell the smoke from the chimney as it tumbles and bounces along the side of the hill. This is one of my great end-of-season pleasures.

A crisp, bright autumnal afternoon spent chopping logs and tinkering with the wood store is about as good as it gets. There are certain basic ground rules when using an axe and it is as well to get someone who knows what they are doing to show you what it's all about when you start. However, my

239

key rules are: 1) to stand with my legs well apart, so that a false blow (if the axe head misses or glances off the log) won't proceed on and go through my legs; 2) to ensure the axe is sharp (it is amazing what a difference that makes); and 3) mostly to use the weight of the axe to do the work, not muscle. Despite this last guideline, the effort required to repeatedly raise the axe is itself capable of tiring one out. In fact, I get sweaty quickly when chopping wood, which is why I hate doing it on a warm day. Finally, if I get too tired I stop because it is often a combination of rushing and fatigue that causes accidents.

With these rules observed, there is no joy quite like that of feeling the axe head pass through a log as if it is cutting through butter, both sides falling neatly off the block. It doesn't always work like that, of course, and recently I have been working through elm, which is beastly and knotted, but it works frequently enough for it to be a most pleasurable distraction. All our logs dry for a season or two so that they don't put soot up our chimneys and so they burn easily and well. I try to have a system in the log store, with the different piles being segregated by age and as to whether they will ultimately serve their purpose in the large fire or in the log burner.

The children love to roast marshmallows at the fire and drink hot chocolate in the evening (who wouldn't?), and sometimes they get a story too. Sybilla likes glühwein and we drink it from time to time throughout the colder months, not just on 5 November. Generally, Seymour spends more time on the sofa as the evenings draw in, and he uses the heat from the embers of the fire through the night; they keep him snug when all around is frosty. I like to curl up and leaf through a paper or fiddle about with a notebook and pencil planning some element of the garden. I love the sight of a frosted garden under a large clear autumnal moon. In this house, only the children enjoy snow.

But even for those of us who surround ourselves with all the joys of the hearth, and determinedly keep our glasses half full, resilience levels wane as winter approaches. Matters that would be small trifles in the summer grow in relevance, even little domestic things. Peverels is at the end of the line for every utility. Our water travels from the mains over almost a mile of another person's land before it reaches us. Our electricity is vulnerable to every storm. Last year, we lost electricity three times during the winter, and this year we have twice already. It is sad to see the last season's berry harvest slowly turn to mush in the freezer.

Our twenty-year-old boiler struggles on unreliably and we have been told it may go at any moment. In among a power and heat outage, Florence decided to put the plug into a sink upstairs and turn the tap on. Half an hour later the electricity to the house shorted and, investigating, I walked into the pantry to see the ceiling partially collapsed and water cascading down, the freezer finally finished off. Throw in a little sleep deprivation and a seasonal cold and there is a hairline between humour and tragedy at such moments. When winter finally comes it can melt this line until it is whisper thin.

Orchard

Above the barn is a small orchard that was productive when we arrived. There are two plum trees; one is ailing and the other is in rude health. It is very important to prune plums only in the summer (not the winter, unlike apples and pears) because they are particularly prone to silver leaf, a fungal infection whose spores are most numerous in the autumn and winter. I suspect many plum trees become infected at the hands of inexperienced gardeners, who check the correct time to prune apples and then march out to the orchard, pruning shears in hand.

The orchard also has several varieties of both cooking and dessert apple. Because they were planted before we arrived, I have no way of knowing for sure which varieties they are. At some point, I will send them to the East Malling Research (EMR) institute for identification – but whatever they are, they mostly taste good. Baked apples, stuffed with raisins or other dried fruit, sprinkled with nutmeg and cinnamon and drizzled with golden syrup is an autumn staple in our household. They are so easy to make. Any plums we can't eat we give away, in little baskets, to friends.

However, the pears are the runaway success and one tree in particular produces fruit of an absolutely exquisite flavour, quite unlike pears I have eaten anywhere else. If I am walking round the garden with a friend, I will encourage them to try one of these pears, but I don't give away baskets of them as I do with the other fruit, except on one occasion when I sent a heart-shaped basket to a friend's mother who was unwell. These pears are highly prized.

You can tell the ripeness of an apple by twisting it gently in the palm of your hand. If it separates easily from the tree you are in luck. If not move on. But with a pear it is better to press the fruit near to where it joins the tree and if it dimples snap it up from the tree so it comes away without half the branch following. Most pears are best after a period in the fruit bowl.

I am afraid the pears are also highly prized by Seymour and, try as I might, without draconian and unsightly measures, I can't stop him from stealing the low-hanging fruit. He sidles up to the tree when my back is turned and in a flash leaps up, to catch a pear in his teeth, before rushing off to consume it in peace, usually hiding somewhere behind a hedge. Luckily for me he is neither tall nor by nature particularly athletic, so everything above chest height is safe.

Apart from another pear, the only tree I have so far added to the orchard is the one most conspicuous by its absence – a gage. I chose the Cambridge gage because it is easy and robust. There is nothing like picking one's way through a punnet of small, sweet gages in the autumn. Like figs, they are taken directly from nature's sweet draw. I don't have either a quince or a medlar, so these are on my very long wish list and, for the time being, if I want them I have to go cap in hand to a friend.

The chief pleasure the orchard gives me is a sort of game I play with the children. It is very simple. We walk around sampling fruits from trees at random. Each child gets a chance to pick a tree, and then a fruit to sample from it. Out comes my pocketknife, and I carefully cut the fruit into five slivers, and everyone munches away merrily, juice running down chins, and then everyone gives the apple or pear an individual score out of ten. This grading is considered and rarely unanimous. And so it goes on. Other than for the obvious culinary reason, I don't quite know why this game is so popular, but I have a hunch that it has something to do with becoming a commentator in one's own right. I have whittled away many, many happy hours with the children this way.

Pruning fruit trees is an art. The only way to get good at it quickly is to go and spend a day with someone locally, who knows what they are doing. That said, generally the idea, as with currants and gooseberries, is to create a goblet shape that allows air to circulate within the centre of the tree and the maximum possible light to reach each fruit, cutting out diseased and crossing wood as you go. As the master cider-maker Norman Stanier says, 'You are farming light and air.'

Everything we do as a species seems conjured from that point where light, air and soil meet. It is the place where our business is done, where we live and where we are buried. We all need calories to keep our neurons flying. Time in the orchard makes me think that we are not as removed from our forebears as we might like to think. This doesn't make me anxious; it makes me profoundly calm.

Perennials

The apparently complicated way of classing plants, along with their often-unpronounceable Latin names, act as a disincentive to people who might otherwise like to get into gardening. A lot of misplaced pomposity has grown up around horticulture. In fact, though the books don't always put it this way, the different groups that plants fall into are relatively easy to understand and there is only one central distinction to grasp. As for pronunciation, there is in fact no correct way to pronounce any Latin name (or for that matter any Latin word) because it is a dead language. By definition, and despite the strongly held opinion of some Latin masters, we simply don't know how it was spoken. So if anyone raises their eyebrows when you struggle through an impossible word, pay them no attention.

If you are just getting into gardening, the first and central division between plants that must be tackled is the distinction between perennials (those that you plant and their roots survive the winter, meaning they come back again year after year) and those that are annuals (which means you plant the seed in the spring and it goes through an entire lifecycle, growing, flowering, setting seed and dying in a single season). However, I prefer to simplify further: perennials' roots survive the winter and annuals' don't. In fact, if you concentrate on what happens to the roots in winter everything else starts to fall into place.

Sooner or later you will meet a third creature: the biennial. If you ask someone about a biennial they are likely to start saying something about the fact that you sow them in the autumn to give them a head start, and they will list a few: foxgloves, wallflowers, parsley, etc. All this is helpful, practical advice but it doesn't help you understand what a biennial actually is. In fact, a biennial is merely a weak perennial. That is to say, it might come back the following year but it might not, and sooner or later its return will become weak and haphazard. In other words, its roots may or may not survive the winter. This is why we start them the autumn before they are expected to perform: to give them a head start.

There is then one final subdivision that matters. Within the perennials there are those plants that keep their top growth through the winter and others that die back to the surface of the soil only to emerge again the following year, known as herbaceous perennials.

Although this may sound like an overwhelmingly obvious point, it is worth saying for the beginner that trees are technically perennials (in fact, the ultimate perennials) and that all plants will flower and set seed in an effort to reproduce themselves.

Accordingly, there are only four categories that you need remember: i) perennials that keep their top growth; ii) perennials that lose their top growth (herbaceous perennials); iii) weak perennials (called biennials) that may or may not keep some top growth; iv) annuals.

Hardiness (hardy, half-hardy, tender, etc.) really just relates to where in the world any given plant comes from and, as a result, how much cold it can take. A hardy plant equals no issues. A half-hardy plant means it can be grown outside but not in frost and a tender plant means just what it says on the tin.

Really, that is it.

Gardening is the home of the patient investor, the one who enjoys the slow and steady accumulation of loveliness in their garden. Perennials do this in spades and for minimum effort. You only have to plant them once and then stand back and enjoy their toddlerdom, their teens and eventually their adulthood. On the other hand, annuals need to be sown in a greenhouse in the spring, fussed over, hardened off and then eventually planted out. Clearly this is more work. For me a larger part of the joy of gardening comes through thinking about the widest possible meaning of the word perennial (a sort of perennial-ism): the idea that, once set, the plant does all the important work of growing and we can just watch. In this sense, a garden is like a self-filling bank account; with a little basic intervention (and, more often, considered non-intervention), majesty accumulates year by year. Gardening is a partnership between us and the soil; stewardship in action.

Snowdrops

I wanted the miniature arboretum to be carpeted with another type of perennial, this time a bulbous one. Some galanthophiles take the whole thing to an extraordinary level. Myriad varieties are marketed, some at tremendous prices (often several hundred pounds for a bulb) on account of their rarity. Fundamentally, I have always believed that snowdrops should be seen en masse. To my mind, there is something sad about a single snowdrop, unless it happens to be in an eggcup on my desk. Of course, planting them out en masse rather mitigates against the benefit of having clumps of rare snowdrops anyway, because they will get drowned out and forgotten about in the general floral melee. Personally, I am content to plant as many of the common snowdrop *Galanthus nivalis* as I can get my hands on. It is an extraordinarily delicate plant and, what is more, often has a lovely sweet scent.

The general advice is that you should plant snowdrops 'in the green'. This means planting clumps after flowering but while the foliage is still green in the spring. This is because they are said to come on unreliably from bulbs planted in the autumn. Actually, I have found they come on perfectly well from bulbs planted in the autumn – so long as you plant them the minute you get back from the nursery and do not let them dry out. If you do let them dry out (or choose old crusty ones that have been stored badly by the nursery) you might not get a single flower from them the following spring. However, the one great advantage of planting them 'in the green' in the spring is that you can see where all the other clumps of snowdrops are and where there are gaps that need plugging. This is, of course, not possible while planting bulbs in the autumn, so if you do intend to plant them then, mark out bare patches with a stick in the spring.

Snowdrop colonies will expand at the rate of about an inch a year. This doesn't sound like a lot but it depends on the circumference of the clump from which they are expanding. In the right conditions (they like dappled sun, such as that provided by a hedge), they will quickly form colossal colonies.

Like primroses, snowdrops are plants of deciduous woodland, and their business is done by the time their taller companions get going. They like moist but well-drained soil and plenty of leaf mulch. Having said that, snowdrops will grow in most of the places you might like to put them in your garden.

There is nothing quite like the sight of great swathes of snowdrops, or carpets of native bluebells, stretching off in a woodland to beyond where you can comfortably ascertain. Everyone should try to experience this as often as they possibly can. If you have children, take them. In my opinion, such experiences are one hallmark of a well-lived life.

Life beyond the harrow

Certain pleasures stand out this year, and one more than any other. The exquisite pleasure of messily eating a perfectly ripe peach. The feel of it; warm, velvety and soft in the palm of my hand, straight off the branch. My first approach: the sheer smell of the thing. Textbooks talk about gardeners choosing an 'exotic', usually a peach, melon or fig, as if, once they have mastered turnips, carrots and lettuce, they are ready to move on to the next level, and then the next. This approach doesn't smell right to me.

As a child I looked to everything as if its growth, its survival, its well-being was dependent in some certain but dimly under-stood way on the strength of my will, perhaps even on my good behaviour. I used to feel all things were somehow my responsibility. I was fastened to a grid of control, a harrow, trying to carry all moments in each single moment; lost in the language of logic; grimly fastened by ropes of responsibility that were fake but strongly felt.

As the brain lurches into being, as it takes stock for the first time of the unpredictable world it finds itself in, this strategy may have some organising merit. It may be a rational response to a recently discovered finitude. In the hands of a forlorn soul it may even contain a fleck of nobility. Nonetheless, a happy mind will see in this nothing but unspeakable nonsense. Rightly so. But it is also anxious existential co-dependence at its most cloying, hidden and dangerous.

Skymeadow has shown me that in the moment a peach is before me there is nothing but the joy of an English grown peach. There is no equivalence between this and a melon or a fig, or a lettuce for that matter. There is no comparison, as if they were children's collectable football cards, or Top Trumps with varying scores. There is no concession to an organising scheme; to a grid of control; there is just a peach, or a child's smile, or the sound of a stick swishing through grass.

Skymeadow has taught me about life on the other side of the harrow. If the eagle taught me that only staring with unflinching eyes slackens the chains to the harrow, slackens them so they might eventually be unhooked, Skymeadow has taught me what the point of unhooking them is. If the language of logic is allowed to run amok, you might miss the point of a peach entirely. In this garden, there is no attempt to hold responsibility for all moments in just one moment. There is no quest for a perfect but thin garden, or a perfect but thin life. There is just a peach, or a child's smile, or the sound of stick swishing through grass.

Skymeadow taught me how to truly enjoy a peach; how to encounter a peach rather than the grid of control that might lie somehow before or beyond it. The lesson has mounted and burgeoned within me directly as I have cultivated this plot. When I arrived, I wasn't listening. I am now. Making the garden has folded the lesson into me, spit by spit.

I think I started to lay out a grid of control, the network of felt but fake responsibility, the harrow, during my very first furlong. That time when I shuttled between two parents, between two places. Both places had precious objects that, like north and south, could never be together. If I had one, I had the problem of the other, always. This is no one's fault; that's not the point. But I attributed the halting flow, the lumpiness, the stodge, not to external physical or emotional circumstances, but to myself. As I grew I attributed all halting flow, all stodge, all confusing feelings, to myself. If twitching, tapping and counting reinforced my newly laid out grid of control, so much the better. My logic was perfect and it worked.

This is the danger with logic. If constructed properly it is always perfect. All you need is an 'A' and a 'B' and a fat equals sign. No one can prove to me that the single beat of a butterfly's wing didn't prevent the collapse of the universe yesterday or that a single look didn't cause plague; such things are beyond the jurisdiction of logic alone. Both statements are patently false, but we don't know this logically. Logic could feasibly support or dismantle either statement. One look in the wrong person's eyes could very probably have led to the outbreak of plague in a medieval village. Logic, as properly conceived and understood by logicians, has a real boundary, it has a hard edge, it is formulaic and like an angry train; it pays no heed to the scenery it cuts through. That is both its blessing and its curse.

Logic estranged can take you to a reasonable solution, or away from one, but it has only its own grinding path. As Chesterton illustrates, someone who is mad, someone who thinks they are being followed by agents of the state, will not

255

change their opinion when the person they think is following them denies the charge and says instead they were on their way to the shop to buy a loaf of bread. A mad person will point out that any self-respecting agent of the state would say just such a thing, and the mad person would be right.

These horrible exchanges can take place in the quietest, most hidden parts of our minds and they can be invisible to others – they often have to be invisible to others – but they steal your life, moment by moment. The harrow; the grid of control; the felt but fake responsibility; the searing anxiety is quite simply a busted flush. We can know this, we don't need to prove it. Each harrow is a trick, a mirage, but poetry has taught me this, digging has taught me this, that place where the finite ground and the infinite sky meet has taught me this; it is the gospel of surrender; neither proof nor logic has played any part in my recovery.

Staring at creation with unblinking eyes works. It has to. It is still bigger than we are. It is still bigger than our hidden places. We can be noble, we can be brave and we can try to be kind but in the end we are in some way fundamentally small. There need be no crazy inflation of self. Grief teaches you this. Farming and gardening teach you this. Working beholden to the season, to the crop, to the fact of the lost or gained harvest, teaches you this. It is a direct cure for anxious co-dependency. It strips it away. There is only acceptance or destruction. Creation retains the power to cleanse in this way; it is a medicine chest for us creatures. If you stare at it for long enough with unblinking eyes, the truth sets you free. I would call this the healing power of a garden.

Whatever I do or do not do, the garden is there. When I think of the infinite sprigs of new growth each spring that happen as I sit at the computer, when I think of the hundreds of creatures, thousands of insects, billions of microbes in the soil, I realise that my ability to influence this garden in any fundamental way, in any way that transcends window dressing, is actually quite limited. My garden places self back in its proper place. My garden has parented me in ways that my own parents couldn't.

And the eagle? It circles above Skymeadow majestically; soaring, watchful and with sharpened talons; ready to sever any harrow, to sever any machinery of control, to pluck out and consume any hidden exchanges, to slay anything that does not bring life. Grief was my parents' last and most important gift to me; they would be truly pleased.

Taking stock

Autumn holds within its essence an invitation to be calm and reflective. Halcyon summer is past and there is something about the softness of the light, the length of the shadows and the fullness of the colour that almost forces you to reflect. The harvest now in, it is as if the season itself calls each farmer to consider what went well that year, what could go better next. Certainly any farmer who fails to take the prompting of the season will be the worse for it, and this is equally true for a gardener. But this sense of quiet reflection builds me up and prepares me for the privations of the season to come. Now is the time to take stock and think strategically.

As I take stock of the last year, a number of things stand out. They come in no particular order. Last year's kittens are now ostensibly cats and there is no question that they have different characters. Collie (the boy, also called Colin the Cat) thinks he is a dog and behaves in a way very similar to Seymour. He is food- and sleep-obsessed and generally, for a cat, quite biddable. His only crime is getting overexcited at feeding time. Pipkin, on the other hand, is wilful and stubborn and will not ever do as she is asked. In fact, she will always do the opposite. She is hard work but, I suppose, charming. Neither of them has learnt to use the cat flap we installed and so the window 'down the back' has to be left open in all weathers.

However, one thing that has been absolutely noticeable this year is that none of my sweet peas or table peas have been bothered by mice either in the coldframes or in the ground. This must be balanced against the lengths of poo that need to be removed from the vegetable beds, the digging of areas into which I have just sown seed and the neatly scalloped mouse and shrew livers that have to be picked up and removed from the floor of the hall immediately adjacent to the front door. The cats give with one paw and take with the other.

This afternoon I was pulling on one of my boots and my foot hit something warm, squishy and mouse-sized. I have had to remove a few mice from the house in the last few days and I am ashamed to say I shrieked and flung off the boot. Celestia (now a toddler) looked at me sideways as if I was a complete wet and said simply, 'Daddy, there is a bad guy in your boot.' She knew. She had planted the springy ball of Play-Doh into it moments before. Things change, but not so much.

Another thing this year has given me is a youngest daughter who, at the age of two-and-a-half, now loves gardening and, specifically, watering. She is genuinely useful with a watering can and we make joint assaults on thirsty plants together. I can't describe how joyful that is. She picks flowers, too, sometimes with a little bit too much gusto.

I am reassessing the importance of water generally, which when it comes to vegetables, I believe is everything. I wasn't helped by the blockage in our water-supply pipe that resulted from an attempt to fix a leak in the neighbouring field last summer. We managed to find and fix the segment of leaking pipe, but in the process some grit entered the system and is now restricting my flow rate to about two and a half gallons a minute (a normal house might have about six and a half gallons), a problematic state of affairs given the scope of our garden operation and the large number of new trees that need watering. I have found ways around the problem, pre-filling containers and adding to the stock of watering cans so one is always filling as the others are in use. Still, it is far from ideal and the structural fault must be sorted this winter.

The garden has focused my mind on water, and particularly the challenge of gardening in this particular climate. I have a feel for it now that goes well beyond what I picked up by merely living here as a boy. The prevailing Atlantic weather system crosses the country from west to east, and spends its moisture as it goes. Evening after evening I sit and hear the weather report tell me it's raining in the west. Here, we are so often left with dry air. In the summer, high-pressure systems sit over the North Sea and suck up warm red air from Africa only to drop sand across the bonnets of our cars. I have heard it whispered at fashionable Essex dinner parties that Essex has the longest coastline of any English county (longer, even, than Cornwall's). Either way, as far as I'm concerned, Essex really is Britain's Riviera: the Costa del Colchester.

So I have learnt little strategies. When I plant out I attend to the way in which I set plants in the ground. I always create a square or circular plateau around the base of plants with

261

edges of raised soil. This means that what rain there is gets caught and directed towards the roots of the plant rather than simply running off. Trees and new hedging plants are vulnerable to drought especially in their first few seasons, before their roots have had a chance to work down into the deeper, more moisture-retentive soil below them. As a result, I have learnt to mulch mine with stones; the bigger, the better. I collect the large pieces of flint that come out of the planting holes I dig for them and I save large stones exactly for this purpose. Not only do I find this helps anchor trees to the side of our windy hill, it also locks in water more effectively than soil alone and looks pretty. This season's new fig trees in the exotic orchard all have a mulch of attractive multicoloured flint at their toes, which I think adds to their exotic appeal. But other newbies have anything from horticultural grit through to old bricks. I mulch my pots with stones too, and as I mentioned I increasingly use plastic pots as a general rule because they conserve water far more efficiently than terracotta.

Many of the new flowerbeds in my garden that are most exposed to the sun also have raised edges. But they are not raised beds in the conventional sense (i.e. with soil filled up to the top of the sides); rather, the raised edges sit six or seven inches proud of soil level. For reasons of budget I usually use painted scaffolding boards, but anything will do. Not only does this act as a barrier to encroaching grass and provide the beds with pleasing structure, it also casts some shading effect around the edges of the flowerbed, easing evaporation from the soil in high summer.

Finally, I have learnt that starting a purposeful weeding regime early in the year will greatly aid the chances of surviving a drought because none of the precious subterranean moisture that has accumulated over the winter will be lost to extraneous weeds. If you can be bothered, grey water (for example from the bath) is fine to use on non-edible plants provided it contains no bleach or disinfectant. Watering cans have been known to emerge from top-floor windows here.

I let the grass go too far this summer. Various work commitments came at me and I let it go further than I have before. I enjoyed letting it go, but I have now renewed the covenant, and I have the hedges before me still. No harm has come of this; I have blessed the insects and completed my deadlines. Increasingly I let things get on with it. I recognise that so often my best course is studied non-intervention. I have accepted the essential wildness of Skymeadow. It will always be there. It is a gift, not a curse.

End of the beginning

Finally, seven hundred and fifty spiky hawthorn whips arrived for the six hundred and fifty feet of new hedge in Skymeadow. I was a little bit annoyed because they had all been packed into cardboard boxes (rather than with their roots wrapped and on a pallet). The delivery company wasn't sure whether I had sufficient hardstanding to receive a pallet. This just increased the need to get them in the ground as quickly as possible, which in turn put me in a bit more of a rush. *Plus ça change.*

I chose a ratio of four or five per yard where I wanted the hedge to be dense and as few as three per yard elsewhere. If the hedge is to be dense at its ankles, you really want no less than four per yard and preferably five. The last major piece of the structural jigsaw in Skymeadow was before me, now I had to get them in the ground.

On the one hand, the sheer scale of the job filled me with dread, not least because (as usual) I had failed to prepare the ground in advance. Usually I would have run landscape fabric down the intended line of the hedge at least six months earlier (preferably a year) in order to kill off the grass. But I hadn't. Moreover, being an organic gardener, spraying the strip with glyphosate was not an option. So before even getting the whips in the ground I had to work my way down the line of the hedge removing turf as I went. I chose to use the spade effectively to cut a line down the middle and then slice out from this line a few spits' worth at a time, peeling the segments away and dropping them back to smother the grass below where they fell. I then worked the trench a bit to loosen up the soil. I planted two staggered lines along the trench.

I managed to get a single row in along main avenue on the day they arrived and then stacked the boxes in a shady corner of the loading bay by the kitchen, stuffed damp newspaper around the whips' roots, and gave them a daily hose down with water until the job was complete. The weather had been exceptional. I was so hot in the meadow planting whips that I took my top off as I worked. This made it slightly awkward when Sybilla turned around the corner with about twelve other mothers who together make up her 'early birds' coffee-morning group. *Poldark* moments are fine if you brandish a twelve-pack. I don't.

As the very last hawthorn whip in Skymeadow went in, and the full six hundred and fifty or so feet of new hedging were complete, I had a very special feeling. As I plunged in the last stake and snapped on the last rabbit guard I stood up and was filled with an overwhelming sense of visual satisfaction. The new hedge is no more than a row of rabbit guards at the moment but I can see how it will, God willing, grow into a definable and permanent structure for Skymeadow.

I had been so busy planting the hedge that other jobs in the garden were crying out. But, as I walked back up to the house, I was struck by how much I have managed to achieve here in just three short years. There is no magic to this, anyone can do it; it turns on how much time and energy you can devote to being a worker ant. I was struck again also by the landscape around Skymeadow and the views it enjoys, and how they lend it truly cathedral-like proportions. It really is a sky-place. With this last structural piece planted I knew the garden could now rise to meet the sky, if not on equal terms, at least as a true garden.

I can't declare completion, and never can when talking about any garden. But, to borrow Churchill's phrase, I am happy to declare if not the beginning of the end, at least the end of the beginning. Building this garden has kept me sane. I needed it to. Endorphins played their part as I shifted ton after ton of soil. But they were a medicine, not a cure. I still pull every weed in a spirit of gratitude.

Looking forward

The only way to describe how I cling on to the garden here is that it feels like a great ship that is being built to some mysterious original plan. The sails have been hoisted, they have filled with their first gust of wind and the ship is lurching forward. I don't know where it will go particularly; and I can't pretend to really have my hand on the tiller, but it is sailing and there is no stopping it.

Ever since our garden at the Chelsea Flower Show, I have found it much easier to sell words. Being a writer is, after all, merely the process of selling words. I have been asked to write in newspapers and magazines and in other smaller publications too. I also get asked to speak from time to time. I don't take any of this for granted. I can't afford to. Taken together it has helped turn the tide, so funds are now at least flowing in both directions rather than just in the wrong one.

People have suggested I open Skymeadow. I am not implacably opposed to this. I would like to share the blessings of Skymeadow with others. We share it together as a family, of course, and with our friends and animals. But who would discover a good book and hold it for themselves, or happen on a great feast and eat it in splendid isolation? If you find a never-ending cookie tree, it is natural to want to share out the cookies. Skymeadow is a rare proposition in the south of England, but more than that this garden, floating in the East Anglian sky, has the ability to soothe the eye and act as a salve for the soul of those who visit.

On the other hand, my family pays some price already for my garden obsession and this price has to be kept reasonable. Assuming anyone wanted to come, if the place was full of visitors all the time the price to my family might become too high. Besides, four children, two dogs, two cats, six chickens and two ducks (not to mention the old badger, whose sett is at the bottom of Skymeadow) do a certain amount of damage to a garden in the normal course of their business. Even if it were possible to balance the division between sharing the garden with others and keeping it for our family, I have one other major structural obstacle to opening Skymeadow: parking.

Until recently, I couldn't see any way of arranging things to cater for cars. I turned the problem over and over in my mind, but just couldn't fix it. It needed new eyes and these arrived along with my brother, Bimbo. He flipped all that I had been thinking around and devised a way of getting anyone who might want to visit safely from a car park, past the house and down into Skymeadow – while still reserving over an acre for us that would be completely private. Even so, this could only ever be one part of the solution, but at least the notion has passed from a troubling dilemma into something that could, possibly, work. It has been said that if you want people to visit a garden you must provide them with 'a view, a loo and a brew'. Skymeadow takes care of the first but is it time to think about the loo and the brew?

This part of Essex used to be called 'corn land'. Like the rest of East Anglia it has always lent itself to arable farming because of its heavy, nutrient-rich soil. One result of our arable heritage still very much in evidence is the numerous Essex barns that pepper the countryside and which were used for grain storage.

These barns are very often, in their own right, buildings of exquisite beauty. They are now invariably painted black, but originally would have been painted brighter colours. Mine plays host to a bewildering variety of insects and birds, including two incredibly plump pigeons. Otherwise, it is slowly declining and we tend to put in it anything that doesn't have a home elsewhere. Might opening the garden provide a sound business case for making some improvements to the barn? Might the barn rise again to welcome the weary traveller in need of a warm drink and a pee? Maybe.

In the meantime I will keep attempting to sell authentically garnered words; as many as I can write; as many as I can sell; as many as the market will buy. The fact of being able to sell even a single word feels rare and astonishing. I am sure it always will. I certainly can't take anything for granted, as is evidenced each month when we do our sums. At the same time, I still have much unfinished business within Skymeadow. There is a new bed whose outline I have dug; it is a hundred feet long and winds down the valley. This is part of a whole new garden room called 'The Suffering of Eve'.

I have recently altered the grass management, too, with the intention of providing areas of tussocky meadow, where I will only renew the covenant every three years. This is to further shelter insects, particularly those that thrive in tussocky meadow. In fact, the garden is increasingly becoming a giant insect hotel – one tiny postage stamp of a life raft within a sea of 'neonics'. Endless worrying headlines emerge from repeated academic studies from around the world that show insect populations are crumbling. Four years without bees; four years?

I also plan an extension to the rose garden and I would like to make a new spring garden too. I would like dearly to treble or quadruple the number of figs in the exotic orchard but fig trees are expensive if bought and slow if grown from cuttings. Increasingly, also, my attention is shifting back in from Skymeadow to the home garden, where a thousand little changes have contributed radically to the overall feel. I am building a greater sense of crowded abundance, of the efficient use of space, such as you would find in a cottage garden. There is a long way to go, but the job is well started. In addition, I must remain committed to the maintenance of all the trees and hedges already planted, clearing weeds and keeping their toes moist.

Either way, I am easy about the garden now. Gardening helped me grieve the loss of both my parents; first, in the toil and tears of the rose garden, and then in its ebullience, abundance and celebration. It helped me as I realised that with a sense of place came something I could share with my parents, despite the fact of their absence. But, while I threw myself at the garden with an unstoppable obsession, the garden for its part gradually presented to me a gospel of surrender, typified by the cairn, the place where the finite land meets the infinite sky; the place where my grief soars still; transformed, powerful, majestic and protective. It was the poetry of surrender that transformed my grief into a sharp-taloned eagle, and it was the poetry of surrender that transformed the searing anxiety of my childhood into a worthy friend.

Epilogue

As the garden has formed around me on an incoming tide, I have seen the pain I felt over losing my parents rescind on an ebbing one. Waving goodbye to this pain doesn't mean forgetting either of them, but rather ensuring they are more clearly remembered. I can think of them easily, even happily now. The garden has given me this gift too. Last autumn, I went up to London to have lunch with Jane Perrone, the erstwhile gardening editor of the *Guardian* and a very kind lady. I went meaning to discuss an idea I had for a show garden but the conversation soon turned to Skymeadow and its story. She encouraged me to write it down, maybe even to write a book.

It is spring again and the birds are singing their crazy ebullient song. The box of fear is long gone, lost to the garden. My wife has her independence and loves her home, my children pester me to go and watch the sunset with them whenever the sky is clear, and all around a lavish, biblical garden grows. I can almost hear it. The picture I bought with the cheque from my grandmother, the one of the boat straining on a rough sea off the coast of Ipswich, sits above the staircase. I see it each morning as I come down to greet the day. When things are easy, it is as well to remember that they weren't always quite so easy. We each have our own exodus to make.

For the first time, this spring, when the anniversary of my parents' death came around three days apart in January, something had moved within me. I looked out of my study window. A robin chirruped. He needed his breakfast. I smiled and picked up my spade. That morning I dug, but for pleasure, not out of pain. That little robin is now tucked up with his little brood in the far ash tree. Life goes on.

Acknowledgements

My work has mostly been conducted in Skymeadow and otherwise in my little study, both of which I am truly grateful for. Blood runs thick where I come from and I would like to call out my elder brother Bimbo and his wife Tasmia for endless and unlimited support of all kinds; without them I doubt Skymeadow would have happened, let alone been written about. But also my siblings Nik, Tim, Nessyah, Amalyah, Jack and Guy along with their respective spouses, mothers and children, and my sister-in-law, Natasha, married to Rupert, and brother-in-law, Julian.

I thank my parents-in-law, Mindy and Simon, for their support in family matters and for horticultural advice. I thank Michael Ward for his unstinting support in all matters; helping marry us, burying my father, christening my son and godfathering my daughter. *Skymeadow*, both the text and my capacity to write it, owes a great debt of gratitude to him. I thank Benjamin Perkins for lighting my interest in the English countryside and for investing so heavily in my childhood.

Mirabelle Galvin for her epic efforts to free modern slaves and, at times, equally epic efforts to inspire, guide and support me. Juliet Sargeant who helped get me going within horticulture. Jane Perrone for publishing my work and for her early encouragement and practical support with this project. Gerard Noel for his sage advice and encouragement. Margaret Wilson for her support and for her stories.

Nick and Anna Milner-Gulland for educational and pastoral services in what seems like a long-forgotten era. James Carleton Paget for dealing with me at university and David Watkin for encouraging me to go there. Nicky and Pippa Gumbel for pastoring over the years.

Georgie Dwerryhouse, Jane Slater, Charlotte Baldwin, Bridget Hunter, Jessica Bond and others in the Colne Valley for stepping in when I was away and our logistical system ground to a halt; without you, our kids wouldn't have gone to school. Bill Cooke for being on hand and doing things on ladders and with drills and saws that are beyond my skill set and would in any case be unwise for me to attempt.

I would also like to thank Claire Chesser at Little, Brown. I could not have wished for a more patient, thoughtful or intelligent editor. Andreas Campomar, also at Little, Brown, who in the first instance spotted something he felt was worthy of progressing and has supported the project ever since.

I thank my mother and father whose raw intelligence and love run through each page of this book. And my children, Isaac, Beatrice, Florence and Celestia, who have tolerated a garden-crazed father.

My greatest thanks go to the blue-eyed girl who bumped into my life and brought in her wake a tide of good sense; for her patience with me and for her Olympian efforts to look after our unruly rabble. Without Sybilla, this book certainly wouldn't have made it to press.